How to Write Stories for Magazines

808.31BAK

Other titles in the Allison & Busby "Writers' Guides" series

Donna Baker

How to
Write Stories
for Magazines

A practical guide

ALLISON & BUSBY

An Allison & Busby book
Published in 1988 by
W. H. Allen & Co. Plc.
26 Grand Union Centre
338 Ladbroke Grove
London W10 5AH

This revised edition published 1991

First published in Great Britain by
Allison and Busby Limited, 1986

British Library Cataloguing in Publication Data:
Baker, Donna
  How to write stories for magazines.
  1. Short story
  I. Title
  808.3′1   PN3373
ISBN 0–85031–701–0

Printed and bound in Great Britain by
Cox & Wyman Ltd, Reading, Berkshire

Contents

1

What is a Short Story?

That might seem to be a silly question. We all know what a short story is. It's a — well, it's a *short story*, for heaven's sake. A story that is, say, up to 5000 words long, perhaps, but more likely in today's markets to be rather less. It tells you about something happening to people. It's not a novel, so it must be a short story.

Right. But it's not quite as easy as that. Recognizing a short story when you read it is one thing; recognizing it *before you actually write it* is quite another. There are certain fundamental differences between a short story and a novel. I have read short stories that were more like articles, stories that ought to have been novels, stories that didn't seem to be about anything at all. (The "literary" short story may appear to come into this category, but in fact its content is usually quite positive, just more subtly elusive. Whether you can write this kind of story or not depends on your own talent and inclination. The "bones" of technique remain similar to the more general short story.)

A short story is not merely a smaller version of a novel. The theme for a novel will not fit into the framework for a short story; it is like trying to cram a mural into the frame of a miniature. And, as in a miniature painting, details need to be sharp. The short story is an illustration of one facet of human nature, generally that moment when a character alters in some way: undergoes some change of attitude to life or to a problem, experiences a development of personality. The story must say something but it is not an attempt to explain the entire meaning of life.

Without this change, however subtle and tiny, readers will be left feeling dissatisfied and wondering what it was all about. They will feel cheated — you have encouraged them to waste time in reading something that has left them no wiser, neither more cheerful nor enlightened, than before. And cheating the reader is something no writer can afford to do. (Your editor won't let you, anyway — she or he will simply send the story back.)

Before starting to write, you should examine carefully the idea you want to express. Is it right for the form? If you have difficulty in deciding this, try seeing your story as a play. Is it a one-act play, fitting into a half-hour slot at the local rep? Or would it need the full two or three acts and a whole evening at the theatre to encompass it?

If there are too many changes of scene, too long a time span, it is probably a novel and won't fit into the framework of a short story, however much you try to squeeze it. But think carefully before you make up your mind. You may not need all those scenes, and a too-long time span may simply mean that you are starting your story in the wrong place. We'll come back to those points later.

Conflict

Most writers will agree that the essence of all story-telling is **conflict**. Without conflict, no reader is going to persevere, however good the writing may be. It is an odd fact that while we like to be happy, and presumably like others to be happy too, we prefer to read about other people having problems. We want to read about the way they deal with those problems. Perhaps it helps us to cope with our own lives; perhaps it is sheer escapism. Whatever the reason, your story must have conflict — though not necessarily desperate tragedy — or it just isn't a story.

Conflict can come in several forms:

1. Conflict between two characters — most common. The romantic story which depends on conflict between the two parties uses the love-is-the-reverse-of-hate concept. Usually, the attraction between them is resisted by one (sometimes both), leading to an antagonism that hides their true feelings. Eventually these can't be hidden any longer and the story is resolved romantically. If you bring in other conflicts too, you can end up with a strong story.

But conflict isn't restricted to romance. There can be plenty of conflict between husband and wife which is nothing to do with romance: differences over money, the children, other relatives, jobs, even an everyday domestic event like papering the walls. You can have conflict between parent and child; conflict between neighbours, from the woman next door to the nation over the border; conflict between authority, or big business, and the "little man". Any of these could produce a powerful story.

2. Conflict with circumstance. Life is going wrong and it may or may not be your main character's fault. In a low-key way, my story "Gnome, Sweet Gnome" (see Chapter 2) falls into this category. But conflict with circumstance can provide a very strong story — think of the unemployment situation, or the bitter feelings engendered by a strike.

3. Inner conflict. The character is fighting with him- or herself, trying to overcome a character flaw or battle with his or her own conscience. Confession stories (see this chapter and Chapter 10) usually come within this bracket, though the conflict may appear to be with someone else.

4. Conflict with the elements. The action story, usually involving a man as the main character. But be sure that you have a strong thread of characterization. Climbing Everest may be thrilling to read about, but only because it is a *person* doing it.

Compare these two brief openings:

(i) The family picnic was a great success. The sun shone, the food was perfect and everybody enjoyed the swimming. The children never squabbled once and even Aunt Mabel and Uncle William didn't find anything to grumble about.

(ii) I shall never forget that day. Everything went wrong from start to finish. The car wouldn't start, Tommy was sick and when we got to the beach the tide was out. I'd forgotten the sandwiches, Fred upset the thermos and Doreen lost her wedding-ring in the sand. And on the way back. . . .

Which one would you read?

Probably, the second one would be written up as a humorous story. But it could be suspense, the wry tone changing at some point to something more sinister. Or the chapter of accidents could lead to something tragic: a bathing accident, perhaps, on that outgoing tide. Whatever you decide, there is certainly more meat there than in the happy family outing where nothing went wrong. There is *conflict*.

Conflict is not, however, enough on its own. It must always lead to that other essential ingredient, the change of attitude or development of character. This doesn't have to be extreme. People don't often change drastically, but they can be making tiny changes in their outlook all the time. That these changes make a story is being illustrated every time you hear someone describe an event which made them think again, or taught them something new. Listen to what friends tell you, take note of the kind of stories you tell them, and you will find that nearly every case contains the essence of a short story. If this is not present, the anecdote becomes boring.

Take that family outing. Suppose the car wouldn't start because it had

11

been neglected, despite constant nagging. The frustration could lead to the forgetting of the sandwiches, Tommy might be sick because he always reacts that way when people start to argue; even the accidents with the thermos and wedding-ring could follow on from the general tension. And what happened on the way back could come as a climax to the whole sorry business — or could show everyone in a suddenly better light, making the characters realize that it wasn't so bad after all, bringing them back to the good humour in which they started.

Almost any human situation provides material for a story. All you have to do is decide whether it is a short story or a novel. The story of a group of people going to university, the interchange of relationships and the changes in them all by the time they take their degrees, is clearly far too complex to be dealt with in anything less than a full-length book. But the story of one girl arriving, knowing nobody, uncertain and a bit homesick, and making her first friend will make a short story. How you treat it is up to you. To me, it could be either tender or humorous, probably both. You may have a better idea.

Summary

1. A short story illustrates *one* facet of human nature.
2. A short story illustrates a *moment of change*.
3. The essence of a short story is *conflict*.
4. There must be a *direct link* between the conflict and the moment of change.

At this point, I think it would be a good idea if we had a short story to look at and refer to throughout the book. The following chapter is an example of a "domestic" short story — not particularly romantic, not particularly exciting, but humorous and, I hope, entertaining. Later, I shall use a story of a different type, also written by myself.

2

"Gnome, Sweet Gnome"

It was at the end of September that Hubert arrived.

He was in the kitchen when I came home: grubby and disreputable, his beard straggling down a dirty waistcoat, and what could only be described as a leer on his wrinkled face.

It came as a shock. Since we'd moved into our dream cottage, everything had gone well. There was a lot to be done, of course, before the dream was fully realized, and I'd been anxious that Rosalind shouldn't overdo things. I was still inclined to treat pregnancy as an illness. And what Rosalind airily called "getting the garden straight" was, to my mind, more like jungle clearance.

But we'd settled down happily into a pattern, and I really looked forward to getting home each evening and doing a bit more decorating. Until Hubert arrived.

"What," I said, stopping dead, "is *that*?"

"It's Hubert. He's rather sweet, isn't he?" Rosalind said. "In a gruesome sort of way," she added hastily as she saw my expression.

"Where on earth did you get it? What's it doing in the kitchen? I suppose you've asked it to supper," I said with heavy irony.

"Now, don't be silly, darling. I found him at the top of the garden. Amongst all those nettles, poor little chap. I just brought him in to clean him up a bit and. . . ." Her voice trailed away.

"And then?" I repeated. "Rosalind, we don't *like* garden gnomes, remember? We think they're twee and pretentious. Get it out of here, Ros. It's not *us*." I peered a bit closer. "It doesn't even have a nice expression."

"Well, would you?" she demanded. "Stuck up there in those nettles. I know we don't like them ourselves, Phil. But somebody might like to give him a home."

"Rosalind," I said, "he — it — is not a lost child. You're anthropomorphizing again. Put it in the dustbin."

But I had to give in, of course. You can't be too hard on women when they're pregnant. And I've always loved Rosalind for her soft heart.

All the same, it was a surprise to find him still in possession of the kitchen next evening. Only now he looked somewhat different.

13

"Don't touch him!" Rosalind cried, running in from the living-room. "He's still wet." She stood beside me, looking fondly — yes, *fondly* — at the grotesque little apparition. "Didn't he come up well?"

"But what have you done?" The question was a mere formality. It was all too clear what she had done. Gone were the grime, the mud, the clinging fronds of nettle. The leer was still there and the beard still reached the middle button of the waistcoat. But the whole effect, though less disreputable, was if possible even more weird; for the entire thing was pink. Pale pink. An instantly recognizable pink.

"That's my primer!" I said.

"I know, darling. I wasn't quite sure if it was the right thing to use, actually. I'll go and see if there's a special paint I should use tomorrow. But he looks better already, doesn't he?"

I sighed. "All right. Get your special paint. Smarten him up. And then — *get rid of him.*"

"Yes, of course," she said, but her fingers, touching the long cap gently to see if it were still wet, seemed almost to be caressing it.

Nothing more was said about gnomes for a few days. I finished decorating the kitchen and moved on to the bathroom. Then, after supper one evening, Rosalind got up and went out of the room. She came back with an odd sort of smile on her face — and the garden gnome in her hands.

"There!" she said. "What do you think?"

I stared. She had certainly wrought a transformation. The gnome shone with cleanliness and colour. His coat was scarlet, his waist-coat yellow, his cap and trousers bright blue. His beard was snowy white and two blue eyes glittered wickedly from the rosy face.

"Isn't he beautiful?" she said proudly, and waited for my answer.

Now, I have never envisaged myself using the word *beautiful* for a garden gnome. But Rosalind's pregnancy was making itself felt now, in morning sickness and heartburn. She was liable to weep at very little provocation. And there was no doubt that she had made a good job of the garden gnome.

"Yes," I said, swallowing my emotion. "Beautiful. Well done, Ros." But if I had known the flood, the torrent, that my words were to undam, maybe I would have risked Rosalind's tears and left them unsaid.

Naturally, I expected that with Hubert now completed, a home would be found for him and life would return to normal. But on the next evening, Ros met me with shining eyes and invited me to guess what had happened today.

"Prince Charles called for coffee?" I hazarded. "You've been invited to compete in the next Olympics. We're having quads. Or — wait a minute — you've got rid of that gnome. That's it, isn't it?" I beamed at her.

She shook her head, laughing. "No — how could I get rid of Hubert, after cleaning him and painting him and everything? He's an old friend now. No; the people who lived here before — not the Browns who left the garden in such a mess, the old couple — well, *they* must have been Hubert's owners. And it wasn't just Hubert. Because what do you suppose I found behind the greenhouse, under a pile of slates?" I shook my head dumbly. "Three more gnomes!" Rosalind said triumphantly. "Little beauties, too. All different. Come and see."

It's being pregnant, I told myself, gazing down at the wrinkled little faces, smeared with cobwebs and slate dust but nevertheless chillingly human. It gives women funny ideas. It's the nesting instinct. She wants something to mother. It'll be all right when the baby's born. Meanwhile, I'll just have to humour her.

These gnomes were apparently named Osbert, Humphrey and Jerome. The next two, discovered in the midst of a holly bush, were Edwin and Albert. Peregrine, a much younger-looking gnome, was found alone standing guard over a drain-cover, and William, Frederick and Joseph turned up behind a pile of wood that had once been a garden shed but had succumbed to one of last winter's gales.

There were now ten gnomes in various stages of restoration, some outside the house, lurking around the kitchen door as if hoping to be fed, the others inside where they were likely to trip up the unwary or slyly smear perfectly good trousers with scarlet or blue paint. I took to walking in wide circles, not easy in a small kitchen, but they still managed to daub me with coloured paint every time I ventured near.

Life began to resemble a secret war. I couldn't let Rosalind see how I hated her protégés; how their wrinkled faces and knowing expressions chilled my blood; how jealousy surged within me each time I caught her loving gaze resting on them. But *they* knew: I swear they did. In certain lights, and when Rosalind wasn't present, a sinister leer would curve their lips. Complacency was implicit in the very way they stood, legs apart, hands in their pockets as if lords of all they surveyed. The fishing gnomes looked as if *they* never went home empty-handed. The gnome with the wheelbarrow (Osbert) could clearly wheelbarrow all day without ever wanting a rest. I began to feel decidedly inferior. But there was nothing I could do about them — at least until the baby was born. After that, I promised myself . . .

During the winter, Rosalind insisted that the gnomes be brought indoors at night. It was cold out there, she explained. The frost might damage them. Leave them out on one of these bitter nights and we might go out to find nothing but a pile of crumbled concrete and plaster. Chance would be a fine thing, I thought sourly as I heaved them all in each evening and stood them around the kitchen. They gazed at me, unwinking but triumphant. And as I gazed back, a suspicion formed in my mind. That one with the yellow jacket and blue cap: which was he? Humphrey? No; Humphrey had a red cap. Jerome? No, he was there with his fishing-rod. Edwin — no. Albert — no. So who *was* he?

"Ros!" I shouted in panic. "There's a strange gnome! An infiltrator! Ros, they're *breeding*!" I didn't stop to wonder about female gnomes. Perhaps they were hermaphrodite. Whatever it was, it was a new and frightening development.

Ros came at a fast waddle.

"There," I said, pointing a shaking hand. "That one. I've never seen him before."

"Oh." Ros turned pink. "That's Stanley. Didn't I tell you about him?"

"No, you did not! Where did he come from? Don't say there's more out there." I glanced fearfully at the kitchen door.

"Well, no," she said, turning pinker still. "Actually, I saw him in the garden shop." She looked up at me appealingly. "He was the only one they had left. He looked so lonely, Phil. And with all these — well, one more or less doesn't really make any difference, does it? They don't eat anything, after all."

"I wouldn't be too sure about that," I said. "Leaving them here in the kitchen night after night — we'll probably come down one morning and find every scrap of food gone." I stopped. She's pregnant, I reminded myself. Some women eat coal. It'll be all right afterwards. I lowered my voice a few decibels and forced a smile. "Stanley, is it? Well, hullo Stanley." Stanley looked back at me impassively. He'd obviously heard all about me from the others, and he wasn't fooled.

Spring came, and saw the gnomes scattered over the garden in various attitudes, some fishing in our tiny pool, some wheelbarrowing, some digging, others just supervising. Of course, no actual work ever got done. It wouldn't have been so bad if it had.

As B-day grew nearer, I fixed them with a malicious eye. Soon, I thought, soon. The garden *would* be ours again. Not long now.

B-day, as forecast by the doctor, came and went. It was a whole extra week before Rosalind woke me in the night to tell me she'd started.

"You're sure?"

"Yes, of course I'm sure. Ring the hospital, darling. Quickly!"

It would be some time before anything much happened, they told me when we reached the hospital. I wanted to be there for the birth, did I? Well, better come back about lunchtime. It wasn't likely that anything would have happened by then.

I spent the morning mooning about the garden. For once, the gnomes did not seem hostile. Their eyes followed me as I roamed amongst them. I could almost detect a spark of sympathy here and there.

"You see," I explained, sitting down on the seat near where Osbert happened to be wheelbarrowing, "we've waited a long time for this baby. And if anything goes wrong now — " Osbert looked wise but said nothing. I tried Stanley and Jerome, who were at the pool practising for when we got the goldfish. They too remained silent, but I left them feeling oddly comforted. I took a mug of coffee out to Humphrey, who didn't drink any but stayed by my side while I let it go cold and talked about the family we'd hoped for. Two of each, we'd thought. But if we were just to have this one — well, that was fine too. Just so long as he — or she — and Rosalind were all right, of course.

At last, I got up to go back to the hospital. The gnomes watched me in silence.

At the hospital, it was all systems go. Things had moved faster than expected, the little nurse told me as I struggled into white overalls and wellingtons and tied the mask over my face. I wondered if Ros would recognize me, but the urgent pressure of her hand told me she had; we were in it together, sharing this tremendous experience, working with each other to bring a new life into the

17

world — and then it was there: a screaming, slippery, purple bundle of fury, bellowing out its rage: strong, lusty, perfect and real. Ros and I stared in wonder and delight.

"A boy," the nurse said, and placed the baby in Ros's arms.

Later on, I saw them both again, in the ward. They'd been cleaned up and put into fresh, pretty nighties. Ros looked more beautiful than I'd ever seen her, and I told her so. Then I looked at our son.

The fury had gone. The sleeping face was wrinkled and elderly. It reminded me of someone. But he was beautiful just the same. I told Ros that, too. Then I went home.

The gnomes were still in the garden, watching anxiously for my return. Their eyes were fixed on me as I parked the car. I could feel their stares as I approached the door. I hesitated; put the key in the lock; then made up my mind and strode into the garden.

"It's all right, fellas!" I shouted, beaming at their worried faces. "Everything's all right! It's a boy! And he looks — " I paused suddenly, remembering that wizened face, those bright blue eyes in the wrinkled red cheeks — "he looks just like you. . . ."

3

Plots

Short stories need plots. Without a plot there is no story.

Plots are probably what new writers worry about most, yet once you have learned to look for them, you will find them everywhere. Your only problem then is knowing how to use them — at one time, it was fashionable to talk about the "36 basic situations" and writers felt that if only they could have this list, their troubles would be over. But they weren't. Knowing about the "situations" didn't turn them into plots. The imagination was still needed, and without that and some understanding of human behaviour, no writer would get very far. (And for this reason I do not intend to give the "list" in this book.)

Plot is story line, the thread on which everything else hangs. Even so, it is not enough to have a good plot — you need the characters for whom that plot will be a natural setting. Plot springs from character, so before you begin your plotting you have to know your characters. Plot and character are interwoven all through the story, developing and changing with each other. What happens depends on the people involved. Forget that at your peril.

Where do plots come from?

How to think up a plot? There are several ways, and using these is not so mechanical a process as it may seem. Don't forget, your emotions are involved too. This is what makes a story uniquely yours.

It is delightful, of course, to have a plot leap into your mind ready made, but that doesn't happen very often. What can happen is an idea — in "Gnome, Sweet Gnome" I read about someone who moved into a house and found a gnome hidden in the jungle of a garden. The idea amused me and I extended it. What if the garden were almost overrun by gnomes, and the new owners hated them?

That wasn't enough on its own. I had to provide conflict by letting one of the partners express an unexpected liking — even affection — for the gnomes. But because I wanted a gentle story, it mustn't be allowed to cause real friction. Rosalind's pregnancy was the answer, together with Philip's rather bemused feelings that she must at all costs be humoured. The conflict remains low-key because it is always tempered by his care for Rosalind.

Nevertheless, conflict there certainly is, and because Philip is a caring husband, he transfers his antagonism to the gnomes and sees them as his enemy. More, he does what he accuses Rosalind of, and turns them into mini-human beings, actively hostile towards himself. Under the happy marriage is a battle being fought between Philip and the gnomes — a battle of which Rosalind seems entirely unaware.

Philip is philosophical about this — once Rosalind returns to normal, he thinks, he will be able to persuade her to get rid of all the gnomes and home will be home again. But meanwhile, he undergoes a subtle change. On the day of the baby's birth, he finds himself turning to the gnomes for comfort. And when he realizes the likeness between the newborn baby and the wrinkled little faces in the garden, he accepts it with a readiness that confirms his change in attitude.

The gnome story is just for fun. But it could be quite different. Suppose there were something really sinister about these little manikins. Suppose they appeared to come to life, though never so that you could actually catch them moving — just enough to create a suspicion. Suppose odd, sinister little happenings began to take place . . . happenings that built up to a horrifying climax. . . . Shivering yet? If you are — go and write it.

Note that all the above story — "Gnome, Sweet Gnome" — came from the characters of Philip and Rosalind. If Rosalind hadn't found pleasure in renovating the gnomes, she wouldn't have developed an affection for them. And Philip implies that she is a gentle, rather sensitive girl who attributes human feelings to animals and inanimate objects. But Philip's character is equally important.

Another man might have sneered at Rosalind's interest, scorned her handiwork, refused to carry the gnomes in at night. Philip, being the kind of man he is, tolerates the gnomes. He looks forward to the day when Rosalind will lose interest — as she surely will when the baby arrives. But the ending implies that Philip has been won over by the gnomes after all. Will he be the one to insist on their remaining? Will he be painting them all and bringing them indoors next winter?

The gnome story would have remained no more than an idea if it had not been for the characters of Philip and Rosalind. I had to know about them before I could begin to write. Good characterization is all-important. A simple plot may tell a better story than the most complex, if the characters themselves are right.

Write it out in big letters and stick it on your wall.

PLOT COMES FROM CHARACTER.

Finding ideas

If you are starting without an idea, look for one. Newspapers are an obvious hunting-ground, especially the chatty ones with lots of human-interest stories. You can't write one up just as it is reported, of course, but there will be few days going by without some little item catching your eye, which can be expanded and built up. Can *you* write a story a day? Collect your ideas and store them.

Magazines are another good source, especially the readers' letters pages and, even more so, the problem pages. There, on the page, is real life, with all its anxieties. The confession story writer (see Chapter 10) will find gold on these pages. Again, you can't use them straight; but as a starting point, with your own imagination getting to work, they are all you need. Better still, they are *contemporary*. And they indicate just what kind of reader the magazine caters for — an ideal market for your story.

Think about characters and how they react to each other, before you even start to wonder about the story. The domineering father with the growing family — how often has he appeared? Three instances spring to mind at once: — *The Barretts of Wimpole Street*, *Spring and Port Wine*, *Hatter's Castle*. None of them short stories, for as a theme this is too big for the form; but you can scale it down to the teenage girl's rebellion against her father's more ordinary authority, and what happens when she defies him and stays out late.

Something unexpected can make a short story; like the sudden revolt of someone who has always seemed placid and amenable, which is the theme of my second story, "The Solution". Take it a stage further, into fantasy — the revolt of an animal or bird. Daphne du Maurier's "The Birds" is a celebrated example of this. And I once read a chilling story about an aspidistra which effectively murdered its owners.

Such stories can be humorous or deeply sinister. But their effectiveness depends on the unexpected twist in the original idea — and on the characters who bring them to life. Even if your main character is a cockroach, he or she must still be a *character* — rounded out, with a personality the reader can recognize and identify with.

If you like this kind of fantasy, try developing other ideas. The teddy-bear who rebels against the brutal treatment meted out by his spoilt and callous young owner. The car, fed up with being neglected. The telephone which rings regularly through the night although nobody is ever actually dialling the number.

Once you begin to think along these lines, the ideas come thick and fast.

Triggers

Look at old stories and twist them round. Nursery rhymes and fairy tales, for instance. I once gave a class of creative writing students an exercise along these lines. Let's see what happened.

First of all, we put Red Riding Hood into jeans and a T-shirt. Instead of sending her off into the forest, we sent her into the jungle of a modern city. What sort of wolf would she be likely to meet?

Our Red Riding Hood met a drug pusher. (We were in a downbeat mood that evening.) Yours might meet an entirely different kind of wolf. And he might not turn out in such a sinister way — you don't have to stick to the story line all the way through, it's only a trigger. So long as it gets you started.

Try it yourself now, with one of the other age-old stories — "Cinderella", perhaps, or "Beauty and the Beast". What happens will depend entirely on you. You might write a romance, or it may turn into suspense. And you don't have to discard a story when you've used it once. Try changing the sexes around, altering the relationships, twisting the end. Ring the changes. You will probably find after a while that you have completely forgotten your original trigger and are absorbed in a wholly new idea.

Another trigger I used with my writing class was to give them all a picture (a Christmas card scene of skaters on a woodland pond) and ask them to write a story around it. The variety of stories that came back the next week was fascinating — from haunting tales of pre-war nostalgia, to suicide (I told you we were a downbeat lot) and tender romance. You too may find this a useful trick. But don't be self-indulgent and give yourself too much choice. Take no more than three pictures at random and set yourself to weave a story from at least one.

When I was writing a lot of confession stories, I was always looking out for new ideas for human situations. A young friend, who found herself pregnant by a boyfriend she had parted from, told me that when her baby was born the Department of Health and Social Security Office had asked for the father's name, even though she did not want help from him and hadn't even told him of the baby's existence. That set me thinking.

Suppose the DHSS wrote to him, not knowing that in the meantime he had himself been killed in a road accident? Suppose his mother opened the letter — what would her reactions be? Disbelief at first, followed by blaming the girl — and then, gradually, the realization that this child was the only grandchild she would ever have. The story finished with her going to see the girl and looking forward to a relationship with her and the baby.

I used this story over and over again. In another version, it was the girl who found out about the accident and realized what the mother must be going through. Yet again, it was the girl who was killed and the boy who felt the need to take his place as the baby's father.

Every story that was written from this basic situation was sold. Naturally, the DHSS weren't involved every time, nor did the feelings of the characters follow the same pattern. But the trigger — a powerful, human situation — was the same. And could be used again in a different type of story.

In that situation, you have all the essential ingredients: the emotion, the change of attitude, the satisfactory ending. It stemmed from one remark made to me, and the rest came from my own imagination.

Six honest men

One of Rudyard Kipling's poems is about "six honest serving men" called What, Why, When, How, Where and Who. Keep these names in mind as you write, and make sure each man has been considered. In other words, tell the reader *who* the story is about; *what* is happening to them; *where* and *when* it is happening; *why*; and *how*.

And if you are still stuck for a plot, write the words down in a column and answer them from the top of your head:

WHO — Cathy, aged 23, infant teacher
WHERE — in school
WHEN — after all the children have left, except for one
WHAT — the child's father arrives, and he and Cathy start talking
WHY — perhaps he's divorced or widowed, and he and Cathy
        become friends
HOW — well, you can answer that for yourself, can't you. . . .

Keep your plots simple — one idea, one conflict, one effect. Discard anything that seems to complicate or elaborate this concept. Light up just one facet of life. If you have more than one idea, you probably have more than one story.

Building Plot From Character

Writers' Circles often get their members to take three or four different nouns — bank manager, wicked uncle, hot chocolate — and write a story around them. This can be fun and result in some appealing stories. But be careful when using these devices. The story must hinge on character. Don't be so desperate to get in your hot chocolate or whatever that you begin to force your characters into moulds they don't fit, or worse still, never let them develop at all. Once you've started to think, you should find new ideas evolving. Let them. Don't push them out — they may be better. The triggers were only there to give you a start, remember?

Let me repeat what I said just now. *The best way to build a story is to start from character itself*. And the more you know about your characters, the stronger and more believable your story will be.

I talked earlier about thinking about your characters and how they react to each other, before even beginning to write your story. Let's consider just what this means.

Take the wicked uncle and the bank manager. Can you write a story about these two people? Of course you can, it's easy. Straight off the top of your head — wicked uncle, fortune to be wrested from a rightful heir, murder of said heir, wicked uncle claims fortune, bank manager smells rat . . . and that took me exactly as long to think out as it did to type the words. The beginnings of a story. And we all know what wicked uncles and bank managers are like. Easy characters to portray.

But what happens if you write the story, knowing no more about your characters than that? I'll tell you. You get stereotyped characters (the "we all know what they're like" characters) going through the motions of a pre-arranged plot, like the puppets they are, dancing to the strings you pull. You get a flat, unmemorable story which will be forgotten as soon as it's read — if indeed it even gets finished.

You might not even finish writing it. Because flat, stereotyped characters are as boring to write as they are to read.

So what do we do about this? How do we evolve real, living characters that breathe and move and leap from the page, straight from your consciousness into your reader's?

Well, one way is to start with *real, living* people. I do this when I run a workshop in story-writing, and the stimulation which I see every time I do this, convinces me that it works. And it can work equally well for you.

You might at first try this out with two or three friends from your local

Writers' Circle, but don't worry if you have to do it alone. By working with other people, you will find that you meet resistance to your ideas and are then forced to think harder about what you are doing — but the ultimate aim is to get you working alone, as writers almost invariably do. You have to learn to resist yourself, to refuse to accept the first, easy, obvious ideas and look for others. You may find this difficult at first — but I never did promise that writing was easy, did I?

Interspersing the "action" by giving short talks on the various aspects of writing a story — which you have in the chapters of this book — I break up my workshop group into smaller groups of three or four. I then ask them to do the following exercises:

* Working individually, think of a person you know well and list all the points about their life that you think have made them the person they are now — their background, education, position in family, any traumatic events, job, marital position and so on. You don't have to like the person and you needn't give their true name — but you do need to know them pretty well.

* Now exchange your notes with the person next to you. No talking as yet: just study the list of characteristics and events, and try to *think* yourself into that person's skin. Why did having a broken leg at the age of ten affect this woman's life so much? Did it affect her chances of getting into a grammar school? And if so, did it make her sour and embittered or more determined to pull herself up by her bootstraps and do well? Can you sympathize with her dislike of the old 11-plus system and understand why she has become such an ardent supporter of the local comprehensive school?

Already a picture is forming in your mind of this person. A picture that is not yet complete — so you may want to ask some questions, to clarify certain points in your mind. And the person who has *your* original character will want to do the same.

* The next step is to tell the rest of your group about the character you have been given. Describe him or her, trying to give a whole picture of that person *as he or she appears to you*. And that's an important point: you will now begin to feel your own, proprietorial interest in this character. He or she has stopped being the real person that your partner knows so well. Instead, a character has begun to evolve in your own mind, a character who will take on an independent life, who is your creation. You won't want to ask questions any more, you will want to explain. You know an enormous amount about this person and you will want to know more. You will begin to feel very interested — and when

25

the writer is interested, the character comes to life.

  * When everyone has taken a turn at describing his or her character, I give them a shock — although they ought to have seen it coming. Take these three or four characters and bring them together in a situation that will make a story. And this is where using the "committee" situation realy scores — because, with no thought at the outset as to what is going to be done with these characters, nobody has tried to manipulate personalities that would blend too easily together. The groups find themselves with wildly disparate characters, living perhaps on opposite sides of the world, folk who would (they argue) *never* meet, never come together. There's no way a story can be made out of these people, none at all. It's impossible.

  But it isn't. And the stories that have evolved out of these workshops never cease to amaze and delight me. They amaze my victims — sorry, students — too. Even those who "only came to give someone a life" or "are really nonfiction writers" find themselves joining in with an eagerness and enthusiasm they had never suspected possible, sometimes taking over altogether. (The noise has to be heard to be believed. We've even had complaints from neighbouring classes.)

  How would you manage with a Russian emigre living in Berlin, an elderly Czechoslovakian refugee living in Britain, a somewhat depraved Oxford don and an Argentinian horse-breeder — yes, at a recent workshop one group did have exactly this mix. They finally evolved a plot set in Berlin, shortly after the fall of the Berlin Wall, and each member of the cast had a convincing reason to be there.

  Another group in the same workshop managed to complete a full storyline and produced a tale about the assassination taking place locally, using local features and events, of a Russian spy; they even ended with a neat twist. (I suggested that they might borrow one of the characters from the previous group to be a "contact" for the spy.) And in front of me, a third group was enacting a road accident, to show how the "caring" character would react in a real emergency.

  And that is the whole point of this exercise — to help writers to understand that the story they write *must* evolve from the characters themselves. Stories happen because people behave in a certain way, because the bank manager and the wicked uncle react according to their own natures. Because a person who may seem caring and in control could turn out to be a mass of insecurities and may panic when a real emergency occurs. Because someone who sems quiet and ineffectual may come to the fore in such an emergency — or may not. Everyone is different.

Everyone reacts in a slightly different way. And so must the characters in your stories.

But they won't do this if you don't know and understand them as thoroughly as possible before you even begin to write. As my workshop sessions show, once you begin to think yourself *into the skin* of a character, you will begin to understand and empathize with him or her. You will begin to see the world through that character's eyes, you will know why he or she reacts in a certain way. Like an actor looking for motivation, you will understand the character from the *inside*, rather than in the superficial way which satisfies so many beginners.

And when your character is as real to you as this, you will write with an authority that will transmit itself through every word you write — and make your character believable to the reader. And a believable character will bring about his or her own believable story. Without manipulation on your part.

Clearly, none of us wants to go into committee every time we want to write a story. But the basic principles remain. Every character in your story must be real to you, as carefully thought-out and well-fleshed as those that evolve during the workshops. Never mind that you're never going to refer to your character's education, family background, broken leg or childhood pet that meant so much. The important point is that you *know* about them, and know the lasting effect they have had.

Listen again to the group discussing — arguing, at times — about their Russian emigre, their Czechoslovakian refugee and their Oxford don. "No, he wouldn't do that. He just wouldn't behave that way, because . . ."

And the operative word is *because*. They knew their character's motivation, they knew his hang-ups, his pleasures, his dislikes. The story had to be true to him — and to every other character used. Once it departed from the truth, a jarring note would be struck. And a jarring note, ignored by the writer, will always be picked up by the reader. You can't get away with it.

To sum up — when you want to write a story, think hard and deep about your characters first. Get to know them thoroughly — jot down notes about their past lives, their attitudes, their virtues and their faults. And then let them strike sparks off each other. Let them develop their story in their own way, and see if you don't get a livelier, more truthful story, which will be vastly more interesting to read, than the puppet-stories that result from mere manipulation of stereotypes.

And I'll be surprised if you don't find it more interesting (although not necessarily easier!) to write, too.

We'll follow this with another story. The idea for this one sprang from something that happened to me — but I won't spoil the end by telling you what it was.

Summary

1. *Plot* springs from *character* — know your characters before beginning to write.
2. *Ideas* are all around you — let them develop and extend.
3. Use *triggers* — real life situations, letters pages, fairy tales, pictures, noun collections, "six honest men".
4. Keep plots *simple*.

4

"The Solution"

"Another motorway pile-up yesterday, I see." Brian's voice had a booming, declamatory quality even at breakfast. "None of them necessary, you know, if only everyone drove with proper care." Peggy watched his hand come out from behind the newspaper, take a slice of toast and disappear again. "Trouble is, nobody does. Drive around like a crowd of complete maniacs." He laid down the newspaper in order to spread the toast with low-fat margarine and reduced-sugar marmalade. "Only way to keep safe is to assume that everyone else is a congenital idiot. That's what I do."

"Yes, dear. I know." Peggy's voice was placid, her response made automatically, one of those expected by her husband. She watched as he finished his breakfast, listened dutifully to his observations on the state of politics, the ethics of transplant surgery and what the government ought to be doing about the latest crisis in the oilfields, and, while he went to the bathroom to clean his teeth, got up to fetch his overcoat and briefcase. When he came back, she was ready with them at the front door.

"That's right, dear." He stood for a moment at the mirror, checking his appearance, tilting his head slightly to one side to admire the effect now that he had been able to give up wearing glasses. One carefully manicured hand smoothed back a wing of grey hair. "Now, what are you planning for supper tonight?"

"I thought a little chicken?" she suggested. "In a white wine sauce, with lemon and tarragon — "

"No onions?" he asked suspiciously, and she shook her head.

"No onions, dear. Of course not. You know I never use onions now."

"And tarragon — that's a herb, isn't it?" He pursed his small mouth. "I'm not keen on too many herbs, you know. Perhaps you'd better forget the sauce — I've been wondering if it's wine that upsets my stomach. Just plain roast chicken would do nicely. With jacket potatoes, of course — no roast. And don't put butter on the vegetables." He shot her another glance. "What vegetables were you thinking of doing? Not cabbage?"

"No, not cabbage," Peggy said with a little sigh. "Broccoli, perhaps, or they've some very nice cauliflower in Hoggetts' — "

He shook his head. "I'd rather you didn't. Carrots and peas, they suit me best. With perhaps a few runner beans. Now, I'll have to be off — got a long drive ahead of me this morning. By the way, I told you about next week, didn't I — an important Regional meeting, have to leave extra early — well, we'll discuss it later, I really haven't time now." He bent his head to give her a dry peck on the cheek. "You might like to give the bathroom an extra-thorough clean today, I noticed some dust around the skirting-board. And the drive needs weeding again — you know how they take over at this time of year if they're left." He was out of the door. "Keys, keys. . . ." Unlocking the garage; disappearing inside.

The sound of the car's engine reached her ears and a moment later the smooth, silvery-grey saloon that carried her husband on his many journeys up and down the motorways slid into view. Peggy went out to close the doors and wave goodbye before going back into the house.

She allowed herself a fresh cup of coffee before starting on the housework, and a quick look through the newspaper that Brian had left behind him. It was her newspaper, this one — he always read it first at breakfast, finishing by denouncing it as gutter press and wondering why she bought the thing, but he took his own with him to read over lunch between appointments. His reading of it to her, whole portions while she ate her cornflakes or kept his coffee-cup supplied, never spoiled it for her. She was always amazed at the interesting snippets he'd missed — the story of the family saved from a fire by their cat mewing outside the bedroom door, the old woman fending off muggers with her umbrella, the forty-year-old romance of a girl who had fallen for a GI who had been sent back to America and only just managed to trace her. Brian never seemed to notice these items. They were probably what caused him to sneer at it and ask why she didn't read a decent paper. But he never did this until he had read it himself.

Peggy finished her coffee and cleared the table. She washed and dried the dishes, tempted as usual to leave them piled on the drainer to dry themselves. But Brian had come back once and caught her doing just that and it had been quite three years before he ceased to remind her each morning to complete the job. For the same reason, she dusted each day — Brian would never let her see him checking up on her, but she had sometimes found clean streaks, as if a finger had been drawn along the dusty surface, when she had omitted a shelf or the sideboard. Today, while she was cleaning the bathroom, she took especial care over the skirting-board, and before she went to the shops she went out with a trowel and an old screwdriver and rooted up the tiny weedlings that Brian had noticed. He was quite right, of course; in no time at all they would have been flourishing. And rather easier to pull up, she thought, straightening her back to survey the immaculate garden.

It was a pity that they never had time to sit in it. Brian was a hard and indefatigable worker, and she supposed that he got his pleasure from driving himself. And, the disloyal thought slipped into her mind, from driving her too. But that wasn't fair — how could he be expected to work so hard when she sat lazing in the sun? Naturally he liked her to do her share, and naturally he expected her to get the same pleasure from doing so.

It was time for lunch and Peggy sat by the window to eat, ready all the time in case Brian should appear unexpectedly. Not that he would *mind* her eating by the window instead of at the table. He would probably think it rather a joke. But his jokes — "little quips", he called them — could go on for rather a long time, and Peggy preferred not to supply him with fresh material for them. She could just imagine the story he would make for his friends out of her eating lunch by the window. "Peggy's turning into one of those old ladies who knows everything that goes on," he would say, his smooth face crinkling like a smiling egg. "A twitch of the lace curtains and you're marked for life. Don't try any funny business in *our* street, I'm warning you!" And it wasn't that she was spying at all; she just liked to sit there, feeling a part of life. People looked at her as they passed, nodded, smiled, waved their hands. Sometimes they even spoke to her when she was outside, in the garden or in the street.

After lunch, Peggy washed and changed to go shopping. Brian always liked her to look nice when she was out. He disliked women in trousers, and she didn't possess a pair of jeans even for gardening, so she put on her blue suit with a frilly-necked white blouse and black patent court shoes. She didn't have a lot of shopping to do, since she'd bought the chicken yesterday, but she liked to go out somewhere during the afternoon, and Brian liked this too. It gave her something to tell him during the evening, something that didn't take too long and could make him feel he was taking an interest in her life before he went on telling her about his.

Banbury House had changed their window and she crossed the

road to look at the displays. Not that she could afford to shop there very often, although Brian liked her to have good-quality clothes. There was, however, nothing in the window today that he would have liked. She stood for quite a long time looking at a pair of slim white jeans, wondering just what it must be like to wear such a garment. She had quite long legs, after all ... and the colourful stripes of the loose T-shirt that topped them, it must make you feel quite a different kind of person to wear something like that. She tried to imagine it and failed.

But it was the dress that really caught her eye. Full and flowing, it was like a shout of gaiety, the earthy slashes of colour — tan and black and gold — jagged and primitive like the claws of a tiger. It was shown twice, on two models, one wearing it loose and billowing, the other with the waist nipped in small and tight with a wide black belt. Either way, it demanded attention, and Peggy knew that it would have suited her. She longed for it, with a quiet desperation, and she knew she could never have it. Brian would hate it.

After a while she turned away, a sigh bowing her shoulders. But she hadn't walked on very far before a shout caught at her attention.

"Hi! Hi, Peggy — it *is* Peggy, isn't it? Peggy Bates?"

Peggy turned and stared. The woman walking quickly along the pavement towards her was a complete stranger — or was she? Where had Peggy seen that long, rangy figure before, dressed surely in just that way with loose, untidy shirt tucked into shabby jeans, fair hair blowing round the grinning face, blue eyes laughing with the surprise and delight of it all? "Peggy, it *is* you! Don't look so astonished — don't you recognize me? Di Henderson? Only it's Di Roberts now. Don't say you don't *remember*! I used to wear great heavy spectacles."

"Oh, yes, of course I do. Whatever are you doing here, Di?" Peggy felt herself at a loss. It was so long since she had had a close friend that she had almost forgotten how to talk to one. Yet Di and she *had* been close friends, hadn't they? At school, hadn't they gone everywhere together, shared their secrets and their homework, giggled over the same jokes, flirted with the same boys . . .? She closed her eyes suddenly. It was another world, one that she didn't even remember very well, a part of her life that had faded almost to disappearance.

"Hey, are you all right?" Di caught at her arm, shook it slightly. "I must say, I don't usually have that effect on people, even if I *haven't* seen them for about twenty years. Peggy, this is marvellous. I thought we'd lost touch for ever. Do you actually *live* here?" Her face gleaming with life and looking, Peggy felt sure, a good ten years younger than it had any right to, was alight with pleasure. "Because I do, too! We've just moved here, and I don't know a soul yet! Look, are you busy? Got an hour or so to spare? Why don't you come home with me and have some tea and a good old natter? We're in a hell of a mess, of course, you know what it's like moving — but if you wait till we're tidy you'll wait for ever!" Her laugh rang out like a peal of bells. "Come on, it isn't far — just got to pick up Jake and Lucy from school, and we can be there in ten minutes. I keep finding new short cuts."

She kept hold of Peggy's arm, talking incessantly as they made their way to the primary school nearby, and Peggy listened in a daze, hardly able to take in what was happening and even forgetting to wonder what Brian might think.

Di had always been her complete opposite, she thought — people had said that was why they were such friends. With Di, Peggy had come out of her shell and never been allowed to creep back inside. Di had given her more than a glimpse of what the outside world was like and she'd enjoyed it, become part of it, made friends and been happy. But then their families had moved; Peggy had found herself alone in a strange town, back inside her shell. It was Brian who had found her there, and for a while she had mistaken his dominating strength for the power that Di had had to draw her out and make her a part of the world. They had been married before she had realized her mistake. She had retreated abruptly into her shell and Brian had made no attempt to draw her out; she had eventually come to the conclusion that he wanted her there.

"Are these yours?" she asked, gazing in delight at the two children, clearly twins, who had rushed from the school gates and flung themselves into Di's arms. Di looked up, her face glowing, and nodded.

"Afraid so. My afterthoughts — the others are nearly grown up. Stephen's at university and Julie's taking her A levels this year. We didn't like moving her, but the Head said she'd done all the important things, it was just a matter of revision now. So we're keeping our fingers crossed. These two — " she flicked her fingers lightly against the boy's cheek — "are just to give me something to do while I wait for old age." She led the way along the street and

33

asked casually: "How many kids have you got, Peg?"

"I haven't got any." She wanted to add *I'm sorry* but had trained herself not to apologize. It wasn't her fault, after all. She hadn't known when Brian married her that he didn't want children. She hadn't known that he would be impervious to all persuasion. She hadn't even known, at the beginning, just what it was going to mean to her: the long aching hours spent alone when she might have been caring for a baby, bringing up children; the hungry pain when she watched the mothers at the school gates or saw the displays of school uniforms in the shops in September; the savage despair that attacked when she was least expecting it . . .

She had never even known why Brian was so against a family. Sometimes she thought that he looked on her as his child, a kind of Peter Pan who would never grow up and leave him. His treatment of her was parental enough: *you'll need your macintosh this afternoon, don't walk along there in your best shoes, have you got a handkerchief.* . . . He would surely have loved having a child to teach, to imbue with his own opinions and prejudices, to control. But children weren't like that now, were they? They didn't remain controllable; they became independent, went their own way, rebelled against authority. . . .

Di's house was just as she might have expected, a glorious chaos of tea-chests and half-arranged furniture. Books lay in piles on the floor or on chairs and tables, so that if you wanted to sit down something had to be moved. In Peggy's case it was a large black cat, who opened a sleepy eye in faint protest and settled down happily on a pile of magazines. The rooms were filled with the throb of pop music being played by a lanky blonde girl who could have been Di twenty-five years ago; she got up when her mother and Peggy came in and turned it down before going to make a pot of tea.

Peggy was fascinated by it all. She sat drinking tea and listening to Di's life story from the moment they had parted, watching the way her family came and went around her like waves around a rock. She thought of the difference when she and Brian had moved to their present house. They had been "straight" within the first week, had the whole place decorated inside three months and not a visitor had set foot inside until it was perfect. Not many had come afterwards, she thought; only Brian's boss and some business colleagues to a dinner-party, and a few of the stiffer neighbours to cocktails once or twice. No friends, or family; the few family members that might have visited all lived too far away, and they had made no new friends since coming here. And not many before, she realized now.

"That was the day I nearly set fire to the kitchen with the chip-pan," Di said reminiscently. "Honestly, Peg, I don't think I'll ever learn. The crazy things I do — Mike says I'm nothing more than an accident looking for somewhere to happen. Did I tell you about the time I nearly blinded myself . . .?" She was off again, telling her story hilariously, while Peggy listened and almost forgot the time.

"Oh — goodness, I must go!" Panic gripped her. "Brian always rings up about this time — he'll wonder what's happened. And I haven't even *started* his supper — it was going to be roast chicken and there isn't time now — it's been lovely to see you again, Di, and I hope you settle in soon but I'll have to go now or — " She cast about frantically for her bag and found it under a bag of hamster food dropped by Lucy.

"Or what?" Di's blue eyes twinkled at her. "What'll he do, stop your leave? Peg, you don't honestly mean he'd *mind* supper being late? Or you not being in at five for his call? Does he *always* ring you at five? And you're always there?" She shook her head disbelievingly. "If it was anyone else, I'd say it was a joke." She uncoiled herself and stood up, holding Peggy by the shoulders and looking searchingly into her face. "Just what have you got yourself into, Peg o' my heart?"

"Nothing." The old nickname brought sudden tears to her eyes. "I'm just — it's just the way things are, that's all. Brian worries about me. It's quite natural. He thinks I'll — I'll — " She floundered to a halt.

"Set the chip-pan on fire?" Di suggested. "Or let the bath overflow? That's not you, Peggy — it's me! I'll have to send Mike round to talk to him, I can see. Tell him what it's really like to live with an incipient disaster area! Well, off you go then. But come round again soon, all right? What about Friday? Or next week? Any time, Peg — and if I'm not in, I always meet the kids from school. We mustn't lose touch again."

"Now, you will be home when I phone, won't you, dear?" Brian said as he got up from the breakfast table. "I was quite worried about you that afternoon last week when you didn't answer at once."

"Yes, dear, I know you were. You said so." Peggy went to fetch his overcoat and briefcase. "I wasn't really very late, though. And it was such a surprise, seeing Di again."

35

"Ye-es." He drew the word out, lips pushed forward judiciously. "Well, of course, I'm pleased for you to have your friends, Peggy, you know that. But you mustn't allow them to come between you and your domestic duties, must you? And I must say, this — Dinah, Diana? — well, I'm not sure that she's likely to be a good influence on you. From what you've told me of your schooldays, she was something of a madcap."

"I won't let her lead me astray, dear. We're older now, after all," Peggy said, and he smiled kindly at her.

"Of course you are. Older and wiser, I hope. And you've got me to look after you now. Well, then — " He began to pat himself all over, checking his pockets. "Wallet, keys, yes, all present and correct. And if you'd just like to check upstairs, dear, to make sure I've got everything. . . . It's surprising what one needs to take just for one night away from home. . . ." Peggy hurried upstairs to check bedroom and bathroom. Clean pyjamas gone, washing and shaving gear, toothbrush and paste, the little boxes and solutions needed for his contact lenses. . . . "Have you got your spare glasses?" she asked, joining him rather breathlessly back in the hall, and he nodded impatiently at the suggestion that he might have forgotten.

"Now, do take care," he instructed her as he went out of the door. "Lock all the doors well before dark, and don't forget the fireguard. I shouldn't mention to anyone that I'm away — you never know whose ears it may reach. I'll phone you at the usual time, and I'll be back tomorrow. Take care." He gave her the dutiful peck. "I just hope there's no contraflow on the motorway this morning, I was held up for over an hour last week. . . ." His voice faded as he went into the garage, and she heard the engine start.

Peggy waited for an hour before she went out. She had her extra cup of coffee and washed up the breakfast things, but this time she left them to dry. She stripped the sheets off the bed and put on new ones — pretty, with a flowered pattern instead of the stern white that Brian preferred. She did no other housework, in spite of the fact that it was the day on which Brian liked his shirts to be washed. She had a bath and washed her hair, even though she had an appointment at the hairdresser's later on that morning. When she left the house, she was wearing a cotton skirt that she hadn't worn since the day she had brought it home, when Brian had pronounced it "a little *young* for you, my dear?"

"Cut short and lightened?" the hairdresser said thoughtfully.

"Mmm. I think that will suit you very well, Madam. It should make quite a lot of difference."

"The white jeans? Oh, yes, Madam has *just* the figure." The assistant's flattering enthusiasm was just enough to prevent Peggy from taking fright at her appearance in the mirror. Not that the enthusiasm was misplaced, or the flattery insincere — but she had never dreamed she could look like *this*. Mind whirling and eyes shining, she asked to try on the dress — the one with the slashes of earthy colour. It suited her, just as she had known it would. Far more than she had dared to hope it would.

Di's house was in its usual state of cheerful chaos, but neither of them worried about it. They closed the door on the shambles and set off in Di's rattling old car for a pub somewhere out in the country and spent the next two hours there, drinking beer in the garden and eating huge ploughman's lunches. Or should it, Peggy asked between giggles, be ploughman's huge lunches? What would have been their English teacher's ruling on the subject?

"She wouldn't have had the faintest idea," Di declared. "The very mention of ploughmen would have been enough to send her into a fit. Have another drink, Peg, only we'll have to make it orange juice or bitter lemon or something this time — I can't turn up at the school gates in a state of intoxication."

From time to time, Peggy thought of Brian on the long journey up the motorway. He didn't expect to arrive at his destination until four, at the earliest — later if there were heavy traffic. The conference would begin this evening and go on next morning, so that everyone could set off for home the same day.

At first, she had worried about those long journeys. But that had been a long time ago. And Brian himself was supremely confident. *Just drive as if everyone else is a raving lunatic*, she heard him saying. *That's the only way to stay alive*. Well, perhaps he was right.

"Coming back for a cup of tea?" Di asked when they had picked up the children. "Or d'you have to be back for that phone call?"

"No. Not today." Peggy smiled, secretly. "I'll come in for a cup of tea, Di."

She didn't hurry. She drank her tea, chatted with the children and Di's husband Mike when he came in. She noticed how affectionately he teased his wife, how at ease with him Di was. He didn't ask her what was for supper or look dismayed when she told him she had been out all day. He kissed her as if he meant it, and kicked aside a pile of cookery books to find somewhere to sit.

Peggy made her way home, still festooned with the shopping she'd left at Di's while they were out. The sun was low in the sky when she finally turned into her own street and saw the police car standing at the gate.

She stopped, feeling suddenly cold; then went on, more slowly.

There were two of them, a big policeman and a girl who couldn't have been much more than twenty. They came forward, asked if she were Mrs Stafford and came into the house with her. And there, they told her about the accident that Brian had had on the motorway; the accident in which he'd driven straight into the back of a heavy lorry and been killed.

"It was about three o'clock this afternoon," the policeman told her. "No reason why it should happen, as far as anyone could tell. It was almost as if he didn't see the lorry in front of him, one of the witnesses said. Almost as if he just didn't see it . . ."

As if he couldn't see it. As if, gradually and inexplicably during the day, his sight had faded; so imperceptibly at first that he might not even have realized what was happening. So painlessly that he hadn't been able to believe it; yet so inexorably that, with the final rapid deterioration, he just hadn't seen the lorry as anything more than a blur.

Peggy wondered if he had stopped somewhere, taken out the contact lenses he was so proud of and replaced them with his ordinary glasses. It wouldn't have made any difference. The solution they had been soaked in overnight would have permeated his corneas so thoroughly that nothing could prevent the swelling, the blindness, the eventual pain. It was only temporary, she knew, but agony while it lasted.

Di had told her all about it — the time when she'd nearly blinded herself by soaking her lenses in cleansing instead of soaking solution. As Peggy had done, last night.

5

Structure

While the plot is what the story is about, structure is equally important in being the way the story is told. We have all heard the joker whose anecdotes invariably fall flat, even though someone else might have us rolling in the aisles with the same tale. This can be due to a number of factors, but the one that concerns us here is **structure**.

Beginning, middle and end

Where does the story start? This is probably one of the most common difficulties encountered by the novice. When does the beginning merge into the middle? And how should it end? It is sometimes difficult to strike a balance between the too-abrupt climax and the ending that trails off into a yawn.

The beginning

Fashions change in writing as in everything else. At one time, you could get away with a leisurely, descriptive beginning. You can't do that now. There isn't the space — stories are no longer 8,000 or 10,000 words in length, they are more likely to be around 3,000 words. And readers are used to films and television, where one picture, seen in a few seconds, will do the work of a thousand words. They're into the action — straight away.

Start your story with the situation as far advanced as possible — as near the end as you can. Obviously, there will have been a build-up to this point — if you are going to start at, or just before, a crisis there must have been events leading up to it. These can be brought in as necessary during the narrative, and we'll look at ways of doing this later.

Beginning in this way gets the story off to a flying start. Something is happening at once, and the reader's interest is caught. It doesn't have to be a dramatic scene; it can be little more than a hint. But it *must catch the readers' attention*. Otherwise, the page will be turned and you'll have lost them. And don't forget, your first reader is the editor who may, or may not, buy your story. You don't want her or him to be your *only* reader.

The first sentence of "Gnome, Sweet Gnome" runs:
"It was at the end of September that Hubert arrived."

The short, one-paragraph sentence is an attention-grabber in itself. Because it stands alone, it assumes an immediate importance. Who is Hubert? He is clearly someone who is going to play a major part in the story. (In fact, he is a token figure, representing all the gnomes who make up between them one composite character.) His arrival is a significant event. Curiosity is aroused and the reader wants to find out more about him.

What he or she finds out doesn't endear Hubert to the reader any more than it does to Philip, who manages to get in quite a lot of background information about himself and Rosalind before it is revealed that Hubert is a garden gnome. By that time, I hope that the reader will be sufficiently interested or amused to read on.

The middle of "Gnome, Sweet Gnome" begins when Philip comes home to find Hubert being painted. From now on he is caught in a landslide, and because of his attitude towards Rosalind there is nothing he can do about it.

In "The Solution", my approach was different. Here, I wanted Brian to set the tone with his bombastic manner and introduce the relationship between him and Peggy. It is essential to give Brian a good, thorough introduction, but I have taken the story as close as possible to Peggy's turning-point, which is when she meets Di. This is the beginning of the end for Brian, but we have to know just why he deserves his fate.

In that first paragraph, we learn several things about him. His voice has "a booming, declamatory quality even at breakfast". So he must be even worse at other times. He likes to lay down the law about what other people should do. When he says that "the only way to keep safe is to assume that everyone else is a congenital idiot" we suspect that he doesn't confine that assumption to driving. And with the emphasis on his low-fat margarine and reduced-sugar marmalade, we know that he likes to take care of himself.

It comes as no surprise later on to find him telling Peggy what she should cook for supper and how she should spend her day.

All this is a development of the beginning, a confirmation of Brian's character, Peggy's submissiveness and the way they interact. But with such a strong character dominating the story, it would be all too easy to let Peggy become vapid and ineffective. So there are a few hints dropped to indicate that Peggy isn't totally subdued. The odd disloyal thought crosses her mind; she still yearns for the clothes and lifestyle that Brian denies her.

The middle of this story begins when she meets Di. We have finished now with the setting, and are ready to go on with the action.

This is also an illustration of the different techniques to be used with different stories. "Gnome, Sweet Gnome" is frothy and fun, a light story that doesn't need much time to tell. In fact, it is all the better for being short. "The Solution" is different. There is humour in it — but it is basically a suspense story. Before we have read half a dozen sentences we are wondering how Peggy can stand this man. Instinctively, we know that she isn't going to put up with him for much longer. The story is going to be about how she gets rid of him — but what will she do?

The reader should not guess until the very last sentence what has happened. (I hope you didn't.) Suspense needs to be built up subtly, and that means you must take a certain amount of time.

It does not, however, mean that you can wander off into description and irrelevant detail. Just as in every other short story, every word must mean something.

A quick glance through a few current magazine stories produced the following beginnings:

A woman receiving a letter.
A woman seeing a man off at a railway station.
A woman on holiday, missing her lover who is not with her.
A happily married woman whose boss has fallen in love with her.

In each, there is promise of action, of something happening. Each is fairly low-key — no drama, no hysterics. But there is sufficient interest to hook the reader into continuing with the story.

What you have to do now is keep up that interest, and hold the reader's attention.

The middle

Middles can take more than one form, depending on what kind of story you are writing. Your story may involve a single conflict, or it may be more complex. Don't let the plot get too complicated, though. Give yourself enough room to write readably and interestingly, and not as if you were presenting a report or précis.

In the middle of "Gnome, Sweet Gnome", the original situation is extended and built up so that as Philip's feelings become more intense it becomes funnier. Philip can do nothing to resolve the situation; because of his initial policy of not upsetting Rosalind, he is in a box and can only

41

play a waiting game. The reader plays it along with him, assuming as he does that once the baby is born the garden gnomes will retreat into obscurity, perhaps even be banished altogether.

But while this is happening, a subtle change is taking place, a change that nobody notices until the very last moment. Philip's first intimation comes as he moons about the garden, waiting for the birth: "For once, the gnomes did not seem hostile." But it is really *his* hostility which has faded. Without noticing it, he has already begun to do what Rosalind does — treat them as understanding beings, at first hostile but now as anxious as he is. And when he returns from the hospital, the gnomes are the first to be told the good news.

Here, the middle has merged into the end with Philip's change in attitude.

"The Solution" has a long middle. We have established the characters of Brian and Peggy and the reader will be aware that this story is going to be about how Peggy finally wins — the worm turning. Her change in attitude begins when she meets Di. She realizes that life can be different and sees clearly for the first time how much Brian dominates her. But she doesn't go straight home and put poison in his coffee. She thinks of a more subtle way of getting rid of him.

It is clear at the start of the second part of the story, when Brian is going off on his business trip, that she has come to some decision. As soon as he is safely gone, she begins to act out of character. Every move she makes is a defiance of Brian and what he would like. When she buys the clothes she knows he would hate — and which the reader will recognize as indicating a very different Peggy underneath — we know that she does not expect Brian to return. Her behaviour during the rest of that day confirms this and builds up **suspense**.

Suspense

The element that both these stories have in common is **suspense**. And you will find this element in every story you read. Without it, nobody would bother to read on.

Suspense is not necessarily wondering *how* the story will end. You may be confident that a romance will fade out with the right characters in each other's arms, a crime story wind up with the baddies getting their comeuppance, a missing-child story see the family reunited, and a

treasure-seeking story finish with treasure found — although it n.
be the treasure that was originally sought.

The point of suspense, in the sense as applied to stories of all kina,
that although the reader may be pretty certain how the story is going w
end, they shouldn't guess how it is going to get there. It is the writer's job
to make that ending — predictable though it may be — seem unlikely, or
even impossible. So John and Janet are obviously meant for each other —
how can they resolve their problems and come together? The perfect
crime has been committed — how can the detective find out the truth?

At this point, the author must gather up all his or her courage and make
things as difficult as possible for their characters. There is no taking the
easy way out. That will result in a story that is weak and ineffectual. Get
your characters into as difficult a situation as you can, and then let them
get themselves out of it. Inevitably, there *is* a way out, and it usually
makes a strong story.

Note that I say *let them get themselves out of it*. The action they take
must come from their own characters as you have already depicted them,
or it will seem contrived. You cannot at this stage reveal new aspects of
their personalities without any previous hint. (See Chapter 7 on Characterization.)

You will notice that all the stories suggested above have happy endings,
and this is true of most stories published in magazines. The ending may
not be a straightforward "happy ever after", but there will nearly always
be a note of optimism. Criminals are not shown gleefully counting their
loot and setting off for a lifetime on the Riviera, and missing children are
not found floating face down in wells. A woman may lose her lover, or a
marriage break up, but the result is seldom a suicide bid. There is always
something else just around the corner.

But the middle of your story can be as tense as you like, provided that
you tackle this with integrity and don't play God with your characters.
Drawing them in harrowing situations just for the sake of sensation is
likely to alienate your reader. And there isn't really room in most short
stories. Touch in emotions lightly, though without glossing over them. In
"The Solution", the reader feels most of the emotion that Peggy must be
feeling. Quite clearly, her life is hell, yet we never see her bemoaning it.
We might almost think she doesn't really mind — until she acts. But
because the reader is feeling indignant on her behalf, her extreme actions
seem quite reasonable.

With the *suspense story* itself, your idea and plot come from the ending — the revelation in that final sentence which is what the story is all about. With "The Solution", my idea came from my own accident with contact lenses, when I did what Di had done and soaked them in the wrong solution. All through the ensuing agony, even when I was convinced I would never see again, my writer's mind was ticking over the various ways in which I could make use of this event. The answer was murder (and that's not a bad title for another story). And it had to be a short story — it wouldn't have stood alone as the basis for a novel.

I was also, when writing it, confident that the method would work — an essential for any story of that kind.

Suspense, then, is the main feature of the middle of a short story. Without suspense of some kind, your reader will turn the page to something more interesting. If it helps, you can call suspense by another name — curiosity. It is curiosity which keeps the reader with you to the end. The same kind of curiosity which makes people eavesdrop on conversations in buses and trains — an interest in other people.

Make your characters interesting people, and the reader will want to know what happens to them.

The end

Just as the beginning must grab the attention straight away, so the end must let the reader go without hanging on to his or her lapel and insisting they are given every last drop of information. It must round the story off in a satisfying way and then bow out gracefully.

Once you have come to the climax of your story, finish it. In a boy-meets-girl story "They got married and lived happily ever after" (or its equivalent) is quite enough — the reader doesn't want to know what the bride wore, where they spent their honeymoon and how many children they had. None of those is relevant to the story you have told. They are assumed, but that is all.

In "Gnome, Sweet Gnome", as soon as the baby is born and Philip's change in attitude confirmed, the story ends. The realization that the baby looks like a gnome is a neat and amusing way to round it off — lots of newborn babies look like gnomes. Without it, the story would have ended tamely and left the reader feeling flat.

In "The Solution", which is told in a more leisurely fashion, the end begins when Peggy sees the police car. At once, we know that whatever she has done was successful and Brian is dead. But we don't know what she has done until the last six words. With those words, the story is told and any further additions would dilute the effect.

Plants

Endings often need some preparation earlier on in the story. These are called "plants" — tiny items of information that may pass unnoticed, but will be recalled later and make the ending seem reasonable and logical.

In "The Solution", I mentioned in the first few paragraphs that Brian didn't need to wear glasses any more, though without saying that he now wore contact lenses. The information was hidden in other references to his vanity and might have been supposed to be part of the illustration of his character.

Later, Di says she *used to wear thick spectacles*. Then she begins to tell Peggy about the time she nearly blinded herself — although we don't hear how. And then, as Brian leaves on his business trip, we get the first mention of contact lenses and the solutions Brian needs to soak and clean them. These hints are all far enough apart to avoid being connected, but when the final revelation is made the reader will remember them.

Even the title of this story is a clue, although its double meaning should escape readers until after they have read it.

In the boy-meets-girl story, if you have two men involved you will probably use an unattractive aspect of one to make the girl realize she prefers the other. Again, you will need to indicate, however lightly, that he may have this characteristic. You can't let it appear suddenly in the last paragraph so that she finds it instantly easy to make up her mind. The reader should be one step ahead — even while wondering how it's all going to turn out.

Curiosity and suspense keep your reader with you until the end. Once you have reached it, wind up the narration as quickly as possible, without being abrupt. Leave the reader with a feeling of satisfaction, of all loose ends neatly tied.

Single- and double-conflict stories

In a short story, you will normally use either one or two conflicts. But beware of this; the second conflict must always be associated with, or stem from, the first. Don't bring in a different problem. That belongs in a different story.

Single-conflict stories are generally short — say up to 2,000 or so words. As the name implies, the story will be about a character facing one problem only, and the way he or she deals with it. The woman receiving a letter, for instance — it may have been from an old flame and stir up memories that are tempting now that she has been happily, but perhaps dully, married for some time. Should she go to meet him or not? The story shows how she arrives at her decision.

Probably, she will end up realizing that she married the right man, and reaching a deeper appreciation of what she has. How this comes about produces the story — a single conflict, the conflict being with herself.

But suppose you want to extend this, give it a fresh twist and bring in a second complication. Why not make the viewpoint character a man — and when he meets his former girlfriend, let her have with her a child whom she says is his. His marriage has been childless, and here suddenly is the son he has always longed for. What is he going to do?

This is clearly a deeper story than the first and will require careful handling. It is a good idea to list the main points of the story, thus:

1. Robert receives a letter or phone call from Jane, suggesting a meeting. He is tempted — his marriage is going through a dull patch. Here, though without laying any stress on the fact, you would mention that his marriage is childless.

2. Robert meets Jane, probably in a restaurant or perhaps a park. To him, this is no more than a mildly exciting event, a slightly daring break from daily routine. But everything changes when Jane introduces Timothy and tells Robert that this is his son.

Now you can do the work. Answer the questions in the rest of the list — as you will see, this gives you the plot too. Again, there is an interweaving of plot, character (we need to know quite a lot about Robert and Jane, as well as about Robert's wife, to know why they have arrived in this situation) and structure.

3. Why has Jane taken this step? Does she intend to ask Robert for help with the boy? Or does she feel that Timothy has the right to know who his father is and meet him, if only once?

4. What is Robert's reaction? Shock and embarrassment, almost certainly — but what then? Remember he is childless, never likely to have

46

a son by his wife. Is he going to be able to walk away and continue his life as before?

5. Robert's feelings about Jane will also need to be explored, and a comparison made with his feelings for his wife. His marriage may be dull at present, but that doesn't mean he no longer loves her.

6. Decision time. Robert, having thought through his situation, makes up his mind what to do. But his decision may produce a second conflict. For instance, if he decides to follow up the relationship, it is going to have a considerable effect on his life, and on his marriage, and we go into a whole new set of questions. If he doesn't, he is bound to have his own inner conflicts to cope with. The resolution of these depends on the kind of man Robert is, and forms the rest of the story.

If you write this as a single-conflict story it may end there, with Robert walking away from Jane and their son and facing the emotions this meeting has brought. It could be ended with a single sentence.

If you extend it by letting Robert continue the relationship, your story is going to be longer and more complex. You may even decide to start it at a later point — perhaps at the meeting itself — and tell the first part in flashback. But the second conflict *must* stem from the first. Don't let Robert wander off into a different problem.

And remember that the second conflict must always be the greater, leading the story on. Robert's dilemma over the discovery of his son is far more important than his original decision to meet Jane. Resolution of the second conflict should solve both.

Setting

Where you set your story is of varying importance. In some stories, it barely matters at all. "The Solution" could take place anywhere, so there is little description other than that which helps the narration to flow. We don't even need a description of Peggy's house — we can guess from her and Brian's characters what it is like.

If your story takes place on a cruise around the Greek Islands, however, you are almost morally bound to let the reader see what the characters are seeing. Apart from the fact that it is an opportunity to bring extra colour and sparkle to your story, it would be cruel not to. And — presumably — your story depends on the setting being either on a cruise liner or in Greece, so it is essential to draw it in, since in this case the setting is almost an extra character.

But don't get so interested in your colourful prose that you forget about the story. Some readers love long, flowing descriptions of exotic islands, mountains, forests and lakes. Others merely skip them. For them, your graphic word-pictures are so much wasted space.

Never forget that you are writing a *short* story. Tell as much as necessary — and no more. Draw in your setting lightly, picking out those aspects which will bring it to life, and then get on with the story.

Flashback

Flashback bothers a lot of new writers, yet it is really quite easy to deal with. The main problem seems to be the pluperfect tense, involving heavy use of the word "had".

First, it is necessary to see where and why one should use flashback. Not all stories benefit from it. Some actively require it.

Confession stories (see Chapter 10) nearly always need a flashback. After being introduced with a crisis — sometimes quite dramatic — which presents the narrator in a poor light, we need to gain the reader's sympathy by explaining just why she or he behaves in this way. An early flashback can impart understanding, gain the reader's attention and make her or him want things to turn out right for the narrator.

This device can also be used during the course of the story, where an explanation of certain events is necessary but would hold up the action. You can relate what has happened much more concisely in flashback, omitting all unnecessary detail. Take your character for a little leap in time, then let her or him think back to what happened in between. You will find it can be done much more succinctly, and it is easier to deal with the time-lapse between events.

As for the "had" problem — don't worry about it at all. Use it in your first sentence of flashback, just once. Then slip back into normal past tense and continue as usual. When you want to come back out of flashback, you simply use another "had" in the last sentence, or give some other little pointer which reminds the reader that he or she is back in the "present".

Have the narrator carrying out some mundane activity — polishing furniture or shelling peas — at the start of the flashback. Then return to it as the narrator returns to the present. Do this too during a long flashback — an occasional brief return to the present will remind the reader of what is going on.

Don't however, get so fond of flashback that you over-use it. Once in a story is all right, twice is getting dangerous. When your readers start to wonder just where they are in time, you are in trouble. Flashback is a powerful device, and should be used sparingly. And if you find it taking up more than a third of any story — stop and ask yourself why.

Bridges and transitions

If your short story is going to cover any lengthy time span, you will need to know how to cope with the transitions — the time between relevant events. As shown above, one way is by the use of flashback. But that isn't always possible, or desirable.

In general, short stories should encompass a short time. "The Solution" does this — we are involved with only two days, about a week apart, in Peggy's life. From her thoughts we learn quite a lot about what has happened before, but we are not shown anything that doesn't pertain to Brian's attitude towards her.

"Gnome, Sweet Gnome" has to take about seven months to transpire because it depends on Rosalind's pregnancy — this is why it was important to name September specifically at the beginning of the story. Obviously, during this time a great many other things would have happened to Philip and Rosalind — they didn't spend *all* their time worrying over garden gnomes — but these are irrelevant to our story and don't have to be mentioned. We are concerned simply with the gnomes.

In "The Solution", very little bridging is needed because the events happen close to each other. The first three-quarters of the story is told chronologically. It ends with Di's invitation to Peggy to come round again soon.

The lapses of time between that day and the following relevant day, about a week later, are indicated by the simple mechanical device of leaving an extra space between the lines. There is no need to say anything like: "It was the following Wednesday . . ." or to make any other mention of the time-gap. The reader will assume this without any problem.

Even in the narrative, where there are tiny lapses of time — the visit to the hairdresser and clothes shop, the gap between lunch at the pub and picking up Di's children — there is no need to mention them. Only strictly relevant details are included, yet the reader has no trouble in deciding what time of day it is. The story is told concisely, almost briefly in contrast with its earlier leisurely tone. But the reader doesn't feel hurried along —

he or she is too anxious to find out what has happened to Brian. Extra detail here would hold them up and be irritating.

The same concise style features in "Gnome, Sweet Gnome". But here we sometimes have to jump several weeks, even months. I have used the extra-space device only once, fairly early on.

The arrival of Hubert has been dealt with fully, since he sets the pace for the rest of the story. After that, gnomes arrive thick and fast, some of them not even getting a description since that would soon begin to pall.

Now the narrative is mostly taken up with Philip's feelings about the gnomes, leading gently into the winter when Rosalind insists on bringing them indoors. And here we have a bridge — from the general routine of heaving them into the kitchen night after night, Philip takes us to a specific occasion when he spots Stanley. And we are reminded too at this point of Rosalind's advancing pregnancy, when she comes "at a fast waddle".

Everything about the gnomes is related to Philip's feelings concerning them. Every word of the story moves it along a little further. If you concentrate on doing this, you will find that explanations as to which day of the week it is, or how long it was since the last event, will become generally unnecessary. When they are essential, weave them into the narrative: "Spring came, and saw the gnomes scattered over the garden . . ." It is what the gnomes are doing that the reader is interested in. The fact that it is spring — equally important, since it means the baby must be due soon — is accepted without remark. It simply slides into the consciousness.

Briefly, then, we may say that structure depends on plot depends on character. The beginning of your story is the hook which draws the reader in. The middle is a taut line of suspense (or curiosity) which never sags and plays them along until the end. And the end should be landed as neatly and quickly as possible, without being abrupt.

One final warning — never, never resort to the device of: "And then I woke up and realized it was all a dream". That went out with Alice. It worked with Alice, because the events in both *Alice in Wonderland* and *Through the Looking Glass* were illogical and dreamlike. But present a logical and highly dramatic story and then tell the reader it was all a dream, and you will never be forgiven. You have cheated your reader. And that is not allowed.

Summary

1. Start your story *as near the end as possible*.

2. Get your reader's attention in the *first paragraph*.

3. Don't let the middle sag — keep the pace going with *suspense*.

4. Express the character's change *subtly*, so that it doesn't come abruptly at the end. Use *plants*.

5. Keep the story concise by using *flashback* and *bridges*.

6. In double-conflict stories, the second conflict must always *stem from* and *be greater than* the first.

7. End your story *as soon as possible* after the moment of change.

6

Viewpoint

In practice, the consideration of Viewpoint — the angle from which the story is told — is likely to come before either structure or plot is fully formed. You will usually know, almost as soon as you get your original idea, whose story this is. This can change, however, as the plot develops, and it is often worth stopping for a moment to reconsider. Maybe the story would be better told from another point of view?

There are several different ways of tackling viewpoint.

First-person

In many ways this is the easiest form, but there can be snags. If you are writing as the narrator — the person the story happened to — you will have to be careful not to let the page get sprinkled with too many "I's", which can look egotistical and off-putting. At the same time, first-person writing must appear more spontaneous than any other form — the writer is *telling* the reader, and the writing should be totally unstilted and natural, as if it were speech.

Get your character's voice firmly into your head so that you can hear her or him speaking all the way through. Read out what you have written — this is always a good idea, but never more important than when writing in the first person.

And if this character has a regional voice, beware — don't tell a whole story in broad dialect, which will not be understood by nine-tenths of the readership. (See Chapter 8 for Dialogue.) Do no more than hint at the dialect, with attention to sentence construction and syntax — or, better still, forget it.

There are other limitations when writing in the first person. Only those events the narrator knows about can be reported — you can't suddenly slip off and tell the reader something this character is unaware of — and she or he must be present during all the important scenes. If something happens "offstage" that your narrator needs to know about, make sure he or she is told by someone else.

If she or he isn't present in important scenes, it may be because the story really belongs to someone else — look at it from that other person's point of view and see.

Having said that, there are also definite advantages. It is easy to see into your narrator's mind and let the reader share all the character's thoughts and feelings, so for an introverted story that involves emotion and stress the first-person is ideal. And it is immediate — the reader gets the impression of being a *confidant*, which is very appealing. In an action story, too, the reader can be "there" much more effectively.

Confession stories are invariably told in the first person. Other magazines need to be analysed for their preferences — see Chapter 10 on Market Study. You may find that they take almost no first-person stories, or about fifty per cent.

"Gnome, Sweet Gnome" was written in the first person. This allowed Philip every opportunity to express his dislike of the gnomes and to add a lot of asides without my having to say "he thought" every time.

But the form would not have suited "The Solution". The suspense depended on the reader *not* knowing everything that was in Peggy's mind.

Third-person

First, you must decide whether you are going to write from the point of view of one person only.

In a short story this is the most commonly used method, and it is not really very different from writing in the first person. In fact, if you are worried about whether you have committed the sin of "switching viewpoint" — that is, *inadvertently* telling the story through the eyes of more than one person — try rewriting your story from an "I" point of view; this will tell you immediately.

Writing in the third person, but from the viewpoint of one character only, imposes the same limitations as writing in the first person. You can still relate only what your character would know. It does, however, set you free to describe your character if you need to, and to characterize her or him more fully. When using the first-person form, characterization is difficult — it can come only from the character's own idea of them, which may not be how others see them. Which form you use can depend solely on this factor — how do you want your character to come across? Does the story even *depend* on that difference?

Using the third-person approach distances you just enough to let you show the character as a separate person, while retaining any secrets that may be necessary. If "The Solution" had been written with Peggy as an "I" character, apart from the fact that the reader would have known far too soon what was in her mind, the story would have come over as hopelessly twee — and her rebellion would have seemed totally unbelievable. Try rewriting it that way yourself and you'll see what I mean. Peggy had to be treated more objectively to succeed.

Sometimes you will read a story that is written in the third person, but from two or more viewpoints. This is more common in the novel, where there is more room and the reader may need to understand several characters, but it does occasionally happen with short stories too.

Be careful with this form. Unless you have very good reasons for doing it, a short story really isn't long enough to establish more than one character in a reader's mind firmly enough for identification. It can be confusing to the reader if it isn't absolutely clear which character's viewpoint is being used, and any confusion is both distracting and irritating.

Inadvertent switching from one viewpoint to another during a story is considered by many writers to be a cardinal sin, and what you see as *using* several viewpoints may be seen by others as doing just that.

This approach can be used more successfully if your story takes the form of letters between two people — it is quite clear then who is telling the "story". But otherwise, I would be very wary.

Narration by a minor character

This is rather outdated — the story "told" by, say, a character in a pub who knew about all the events but took either a very small part or no part at all in them. It often involves heavy use of dialect (see Chapter 8). Most of these stories would be better tidied up by dropping the narrator and the dialect and told in the usual way.

However, you can sometimes use a minor character to tell a story, provided you follow these rules:

Your minor character should add something of his or her own — humour, perhaps, or a child's innocence as to the real meaning of what he or she relates.

Your "minor" character should turn out to play a key role in the story — perhaps some innocent action of theirs changes the whole course of events, without their even realizing it.

Little Josephine's view of her big sister's stormy romance will be less than interesting — unless it is by some inadvertent action of hers that the star-crossed lovers come together again. Even better if it was her fault they parted in the first place. The reader will see what Josephine does not, and enjoy it all the more.

Viewpoint can change the whole character of a story. Everyone views the same events in different ways, and each of your characters will have a different story to tell. Look carefully at them and decide which is the most interesting.

I wrote a story about a grandfather who lost contact with his grandchild after the death of his daughter — he had never got on with his son-in-law and communication stopped. After a while, events helped the young man to realize that he was depriving his child of a grandparent and he resumed contact.

The story was returned to me with the remark that this was really the son-in-law's story — which it was, since he was the one who had changed. I rewrote it, sent it back and it was accepted.

Rewritten to show the grandfather as the one whose attitude had changed, it might be taken by a magazine aimed at retired people. Or I could write it from the point of view of the child when a few years older, sending it to a teenage magazine. But in each story I would have to make sure that it was my viewpoint character who changed in some way. Perhaps the old man blamed his son-in-law for the accident which killed his daughter, and had to overcome this feeling before the family could get together again. Or in the case of the teenager, maybe he had felt slighted and neglected by his grandfather, until something helped him to understand the effects of grief.

Don't be too quick to decide who is to be your viewpoint character, and how he or she should be presented. Give it as much thought as you give to the rest of the story.

Summary

1. Decide who is the *main character* — i.e. the person undergoing a change — and tell the story through the eyes of that character.
2. Keep to *one viewpoint only* throughout the story.
3. Don't be afraid to break these rules — but only with *good reason*!

7

Characterization

The interest a reader has in a short story depends almost entirely upon the characters. The most dramatic and ingenious plot will not keep your reader interested if the characters are not believable.

And since plot comes from character, your characters must clearly be your first consideration after the original idea.

Ideas from characters

Characters can even supply you with the idea. This wasn't what happened in either of my stories, since for both the idea came first. But what about the Red Riding Hood story my class dreamed up? Didn't that come first from the character of the innocent girl, going out into the modern city jungle?

We all had a picture in our minds of Red Riding Hood (or Sharon or Tracy, as she would probably have been called). We saw her as an ordinary girl who hadn't much experience of the world and was likely to fall foul of any wolves she might meet. At this point, we would have stopped to think through her character, so that we would have known what her reactions were likely to be when she came into contact with the drug-pusher.

We would have had to consider the pusher's character too — what kind of person would be able to persuade a young girl to start on drugs? Presumably he would have to appear superficially attractive. If we liked, we could go deeper still and wonder why he was doing this, so that his character would soon become at least as important as Sharon's.

Think of a few other characters you could weave stories around. The domineering father — I am willing to bet that with just two words a picture of him has sprung into your mind. Think about his life, what he does, what kind of family he has . . . isn't the germ of an idea already forming? Write it down. You may have a story.

The harassed housewife, at the end of her tether. . . . The typist on the bus. . . . The marathon runner. . . . The elderly woman living alone. . . . You can find a story for each of these characters simply by thinking about their lives. And there is no need ever to run out of characters, for they are all around us every day. All you need to do is go out and watch. Take a bus ride, sit in a café — and keep your eyes and ears wide, wide open.

The reader needs quite a lot of help to see the character you have in mind, and if the reader doesn't see the same person, your story is going to be in trouble from the start. There is even less likelihood of the reader seeing that person if you're not too clear about him or her yourself. So you have to know quite a lot about your character before you begin — more than you are ever going to tell your reader. But until you write the story, how do you know just what you need to say?

Let's look at Sharon again. A fairly typical teenager, with a normal home background. A bit shy and unsure (yes, there *are* plenty of teenagers like that!) but she's just beginning to leave childhood behind and grope towards independence.

Maybe she has just tried out a new, punky hairstyle for the first time, causing a mild sensation at home. Feeling a mixture of extra confidence because of her mates' reactions, together with a rebellious defiance brought about by her family's, she sets out to go to a party, perhaps given by someone she doesn't know very well. The new hairstyle is an attempt to be one of a crowd she hasn't previously mixed with very much.

Why is Sharon so uncertain of herself? What sort of family does she come from? Is she an only child, with over-protective parents? Or perhaps the youngest, forever trying to keep up with older brothers and sisters? Or maybe she has just one sister and they are rivals. Think about what kind of family background would produce this naive teenager who looks like a dream for the drug-peddler.

She may not, of course, be such easy game as he imagines. Something in her background may have given her a strength she doesn't even suspect so that when the crunch comes she can stand up for herself, see sense and refuse to be drawn into his net. The story could end with her leaving the party, less naive than when she arrived but also more confident. This time her confidence comes not from a spiky pink hairdo but from knowing that she is, after all, a strong person, able to look after herself.

This story could be treated in several different ways. As a confession story it would be told by Sharon herself, ending with her realization that although this time she coped, there is good reason for her family's concern for her. She will probably have developed a closer understanding of her parents and an appreciation of their standards.

A different kind of teenage magazine would probably take a story like this, too, treated fairly lightly but without playing down the dangers Sharon faces. It would be similar to the confession story, but needn't be told by Sharon herself.

Or you might sell it to a magazine published for the older woman — the reader who might herself have teenage children. Seeing Sharon as an apparently wayward, punky teenager, who is basically shy and uncertain yet still able to tell right from wrong, might reassure a lot of mothers, while helping them to realize that children do have to grow up and face their own dangers.

And all this from one fairy-tale! But it wouldn't have come about if we hadn't started to think about Sharon herself — our main character.

Getting your character over

Having got your character firmly fixed in your mind, your job now is to express him or her to your reader. You want the reader to see the character as you do — as domineering, funny, pathetic, lovable. If this doesn't happen, the story won't work.

Don't let yourself get carried away by characters and introduce a whole crowd of them. Controlling a lot of people in a story is not easy, even if they all have an important part to play. (If they don't, they shouldn't be in the story at all.) Even then, they may be needed only as tiny bit-part players — like the hairdresser and shop assistant in "The Solution". They were necessary to move the action along and show what Peggy was doing without merely reporting it, but as characters they had no existence. With characters like these, pay them as little attention as possible and never give them names. This allows them to slip past the reader's consciousness without impinging on it.

In a short story, the reader is generally interested in only those characteristics which are relevant, and make the character believable. Your harassed housewife may be passionately fond of stick insects, but unless it affects the story we don't need to say so. Peggy may well have loved to spend her evenings doing tapestry, or Philip been keen on photography, but neither characteristic would have improved the story.

Physical description

Characters in a short story should be outlined firmly, with as few strokes as possible, like a cartoon. Don't go in for a lot of physical description — pick on one or two aspects which will draw the whole picture. I recently read a description of George I at his coronation — "frog-eyed and corpulent". Doesn't that say it all? Or try something like: "He reminded me of a pin — long and thin, with a little round head. And every bit as sharp." Do you really need to say more about this character?

Looking through my own two stories I notice that I have used almost no physical description, except for the gnomes themselves. With Hubert, it was essential, but in his case the description was intended to mislead the reader into supposing that he was a human being — a tramp, perhaps, or a particularly disreputable relative.

Hubert is described at every stage of his transformation because it is essential to the story. But the other gnomes are barely described at all, except when Stanley makes his appearance. Clearly, they are all different — even Philip knows each one by name. But the reader doesn't need individual descriptions; they would hold up the story and quickly become boring.

I have used a little more physical description in "The Solution". Brian "purses his small mouth" and Di is presented as a casual, untidy but warm figure. Peggy is described more subtly by the contrast between the clothes she actually wears (because Brian likes them) and the clothes she longs for. By these, we know that a different Peggy lurks underneath and we hope that she can be set free.

What people wear is often as useful as physical description in getting a character across. A boss might see his secretary almost entirely in terms of what she wears: "Rebecca was wearing black that day; a soft, clinging sort of black that hinted disturbingly but never told the whole story." At once we get an idea of the characters of both Rebecca and her boss.

The progress of a repressed woman might be charted by what she wears, beginning in fitted suits and plain shoes, going on to buy lacy underwear, and reaching liberation when she appears in something much more daring. Clothes are a statement about ourselves; make use of this fact, though you will never need to draw the reader's attention to what you are doing. Your description of a girl in a low-cut red velvet dress will tell your readers what you want them to know about her.

Don't forget accessories like spectacles, bags, wallets. Is your character the kind of man who uses a purse — and what kind of man *is* that? The glasses a person wears can give character clues too. Plain, rimless ones will hint at someone who is both thoughtful and practical. Flamboyant fashion specs declare a girl who likes to keep up with the times and isn't worried about other people's reactions. Big, owlish, horn-rimmed glasses will be worn by a man who doesn't feel the need to hide his flaws.

Keeping a character alive

The first introduction of a character is clearly important in getting him or her across to the reader, and any outstanding characteristic, or "marker", should be used then. But don't leave it at that. You should be reinforcing your character right through the story, not always with the same marker but with different little hints that will gradually build him or her up. Without labouring the point, make him or her a real person every time they move or speak. Don't let them fade away into cardboard.

In "Gnome, Sweet Gnome", Philip is constant in both his care for Rosalind and his dislike of the gnomes. He projects a kind of "mass character" on to the gnomes which the reader accepts even while laughing at it.

In "The Solution", Brian's character comes over with every word he speaks. From the first sentence, we know that he is bombastic and conceited. Within a few paragraphs we see him treating his wife like a four-year-old imbecile. He is also physically rather vain — which is probably why he has recently changed to contact lenses. That's enough. It's all we need to help us sympathize with Peggy, and we don't need to know whether he is equally bullying with his secretary, hated by all his colleagues or disliked by the few friends he and Peggy have. We can fill in those details for ourselves.

Peggy comes over by her placid voice and dutiful listening as a gentle, submissive wife. But there are occasional hints that she doesn't succumb altogether willingly to Brian's bullying. When she does something he wouldn't like — such as eating at the window — she watches out for Brian, because she intends to do what she enjoys but prefers to avoid the consequences. Peggy likes a quiet life, it is clear; but is she going to tolerate Brian's domineering ways for ever? She hasn't always been so submissive, as we see from her conversation with Di. Here is a worm that is ready to turn, and the reader wants to know how.

You can describe characters by appearance, by behaviour, by what they say and the way they say it. You can also use movement — a person's stance and walk are highly characteristic — gestures and mannerisms. Don't overdo these and become repetitive. A hero who is constantly running his fingers through his hair will appear frenetic, a girl who is forever repairing her make-up will seem vain and shallow. If you want her to be vain and shallow, of course, that's fine. But vary the ways in which she shows it.

Summary

1. Characters give you stories.
2. *Know* your characters — if you can't picture them, neither will your reader.
3. Don't give names to "bit-part" characters.
4. Keep numbers to a minimum. Don't introduce irrelevant characters.
5. Don't overdo physical description — pick out one or two features and make them memorable.
6. Use clothes as a statement of character.
7. Use movement, mannerisms and tricks of speech to establish character.
8. Spread characterization throughout the story.

8

Dialogue

Dialogue is supremely important in short stories.

Some people will decide whether or not to read a story simply on the basis of how much dialogue it contains. Those brief paragraphs, often no more than a single sentence or even just one word, surrounded by quotation marks, impart to the page a lively look that is almost irresistible. They give the impression of action — something happening between two people. Maybe it's an argument, maybe they're falling in love — which is it? Curiosity is aroused and the reader starts to read.

On the other hand, the device of using *only* dialogue is to be treated with care, and is probably not for the beginner to try. If you do write like that — well, maybe you should be writing plays. Most short stories do require some narrative.

Part of the appeal of dialogue is that it is easier to read and often moves the story along more quickly. Narrative in the third person is inevitably more formal. Less dialogue may be necessary if you are narrating in the first person, which will entail a much chattier, more colloquial style throughout. Confession stories often include less dialogue, being told so much through the narrator's thoughts — but even so, you should try to include as much as possible, to break up large blocks of narration.

In the two story examples in this book, there is a mix of dialogue and narrative. I didn't analyse how much when I was writing them, I just did what "felt right". But looking at them now, I see that in "Gnome, Sweet Gnome", which is told in the first person, 500 of the 2,100 words are dialogue — just under a quarter. In "The Solution" which is 4,000 words long, there are 1500 words of dialogue — well over a quarter. But few of them are spoken by the main character, Peggy. She is a quiet person and most of her responses to Brian and Di are in thought.

The dialogue of the other two is quite different. Brian speaks in pompous tones, his words and phrases heavy and dictatorial. Di speaks quickly, information tumbling from her lips. As it happens, they never meet so never speak together, but if they did it would be clear from what is said, and how, just which character is speaking.

Listen to the way people talk. Everyone has his or her own speech mannerisms, favourite sayings and idiom, odd little tricks of syntax or pronunciation. All these can be employed to differentiate between characters and give them a flavour of their own when speaking.

Characters should all have their own "tone of voice". Except for short remarks (like "yes" and "no") the reader should be able to tell who is speaking without the author's intervention. And it should be possible to understand *how* the dialogue is spoken, too, without recourse to too many adverbs.

There are a lot of ways of saying things — loudly, quietly, angrily, passionately, soulfully, gently, harshly . . . the list is almost endless. But too many adverbs will make your dialogue look ridiculous. I once counted twelve adverbs on one page of dialogue in a book, each denoting an apparent change in emotion, so that I was left with a picture of two manic-depressives in overdrive.

You can sometimes turn words around so that an adverb is implied — "he said without heat", for instance, may be better than "coolly". Again it is a device not to be over-used. Words count in a short story.

Don't get carried away by the many ways of saying "said". A character can cry, exclaim, ejaculate, mutter, mumble, gasp, shout, bellow, or utter — to mention but a few. And it adds interest to use a different word occasionally. But too many will, just like the adverbs, seem overdone and detract from the story. Don't forget, it is the story that is paramount, not your extensive vocabulary. Keep it simple and direct.

If the dialogue itself is right, there should be little need either for adverbs or over-colourful verbs. Then, when you do use one, it will have maximum impact.

Colourful dialogue

In the first exchange with Rosalind, Philip's emotions on seeing Hubert are indicated by his "stopping dead" as he asks what it is. Notice how breaking this short sentence gives it added strength. I didn't use the verb "ask" here; he knows very well it's a garden gnome. What he is really asking is what it's doing in the kitchen.

Rosalind answers him, then catches Philip's expression (which doesn't need to be described to the reader) and adds "hastily".

Philip replies "with heavy irony" — not "ironically", which would have had slightly less emphasis.

Rosalind's reply "trails away" but Philip catches her last words and repeats them. There is no need to tell the reader how he is speaking — his words and reactions make it obvious.

Read the dialogue from that point. Apart from the occasional "demanded" or "cried", I have used mostly "said", or else left the dialogue without indications as to who is speaking. Dialogue is also woven in with action, as when Rosalind comes running in from the living-room to admire the pink Hubert.

You don't need to indicate who is speaking by using a speech verb every time. Mention of a character immediately before or after speech, according to need (a character who hasn't spoken for a while will need to be introduced first) will show the reader whose voice to listen to:

"John stubbed out his cigarette. 'If you want my opinion, the whole thing's nonsense.' "

The reader knows it is John speaking. Or try it the other way around:

" 'If you want my opinion — ' John stubbed out his cigarette — 'the whole thing's nonsense.' "

It works just as well. It is for you to decide which way works best in any situation.

Break up long patches of dialogue with brief snatches of narrative. People don't generally stand and make speeches at each other. They move about, fidget, carry on with a job. Show this happening, as with Brian's speech which is the opening paragraph in "The Solution". By the time the reader has finished reading it, he or she has a complete picture of Brian at the breakfast table as well as a good idea of his character.

Accents and dialect

Not everybody speaks Received English, and you will often want to depict a character who has either a regional or foreign accent, or speaks in dialect. This is a tricky area, but probably easier today than it has ever been.

Old-fashioned novels and stories are full of characters who seem to speak some secret language of their own, which can take hours of deciphering before you discover that they are actually speaking regional English. Cockneys, Scotsmen, Cornishmen, Irishmen — all seem to be using different words with unrecognizable spellings. You have to say them out loud to get any idea of what they mean, and even then it often remains obscure. And foreigners are even worse!

Misspelt words, denoting an accent, are much less used now. With the opportunity of hearing a wide variety of accents every day on radio and television, most of us are familiar with the way a Geordie speaks, for example, or a Welshman. You need no more than a hint in the first sentence or two. You can leave it to readers to supply the detail — if they want to. What is more important is the construction of sentences.

Listen to regional characters in radio and TV plays. Listen to the local voices around your own home. You have probably already noticed that they use different constructions, different syntax. This is how you should present your character in print.

There are local colloquialisms, too. We are all familiar with the "ee, bah gum" of the stereotyped Yorkshireman. But do they really say this in Yorkshire? Isn't there some other saying you could use instead? Something that most people haven't consciously noticed but will immediately recognize as ringing true?

Try to hear the character's voice in your head as you write, and you will find that the appropriate cadences are finding their way on to the page. You may see little difference in the words — but read them in the same way, hearing the words as if they were spoken, and the Welsh lilt or the Cornish brogue reaffirms itself. And they will do the same with your reader, without distracting his or her attention.

Do your characters drop their aitches? This seems to bother almost every writer at some time. If you drop them all, the page soon begins to look as if someone has spilt a jar of tadpoles over it. Can you simply drop one or two and then return to conventional spelling? Drop those on more important words, letting the lesser ones slip through? Or would it be better to indicate the accent (it seems to be mostly Cockney that presents this problem) in some other way?

Try several different ways, to see which works best for you. It will often depend on what you have already written, or are going to write next.

If your character is going to do a lot of talking, devices that rely too much on misspellings or punctuation will become very irritating. Use other speech mannerisms as well, to vary the pace and strike a better balance. The use of "me" for "my". A sprinkling of Cockney slang — provided the reader in Timbuctoo can understand it. The different use of grammar (such as the double negative) which often occurs in regional speech.

Here, to illustrate several different methods of using speech as part of characterization, is an extract from one of my books, which could equally be used as part of a short story (the book was written in short, episodical chapters which often stood alone).

Old Harry is a down-and-out, attending a local jumble sale:

Harry waited patiently. Now that someone else was doing the searching for him, he felt entitled to hand over the responsibility for finding himself a pair of boots. With the mild interest that passed with him for excitement, he let his eyes wander over the pile of shoes and boots. It was an education what people would wear on their feet these days. Look at them sandals, no more than a few bits of string and a sole. And that pair of clogs. Mill girls used to wear them in Lancashire, he knew that, and just lately he'd seen young girls in this very town wearing them, girls who'd never been near a mill. Didn't seem to be any sense in it. A good pair of boots was what you wanted, keep the wet out and keep your feet warm in winter.

"Ah — I thought I'd seen them."

She was holding up a pair now, just what he wanted. Good strong boots, with heavy soles and long laces. He reached over for them.

"Try one." She was keeping a good hold of the other one, thought he'd try to make away with them without paying. He bent and slid it on to his foot, his grimy face splitting with pleasure as he felt the comfort of good, strong leather.

"They'll do a treat, Missus. I'll take 'em."

"Fifty pence," she said, and his face fell.

"Fifty! I'd 'oped to get ɔ jacket as well."

The woman looked at him and hesitated. He saw her eyes on his unwashed whiskers, dilapidated jacket and overcoat.

"Well . . . I don't know. It's for charity, you see."

"Charity?"

"It's for the old folk," she explained. "For their outing." She fiddled with the remaining boot, a slight flush on her powdered cheeks.

"Tell you what, then," Old Harry said with a sudden burst of generosity, "you let me 'ave these boots for twenty pence and I'll give you me old ones in part-exchange. Can't say fairer than that, now can I?"

He handed the money and the damp, stinking boots, still with their padding of sodden newspaper, over the stall and took the new one from her unresisting hands. In a moment, it was on his foot; and Old Harry, showing more alacrity than he had for weeks, was swallowed up and lost in the increasing tide of bargain hunters.

In this extract, Old Harry is shown as having an uneducated command of English. The dialogue overlaps into his thoughts and when this happens the narrative slips easily into his vernacular. The dropped aitch 'appens — sorry — much less often than one might expect; in several cases I was able to avoid it by using a word that didn't begin with "h". But I didn't use it when presenting his thoughts as part of the narrative; only sentence construction was necessary to indicate that it was Harry thinking. It was the same with other characters used as viewpoint characters during the book.

It really boils down to the same principle: know your characters. If you have a really full, rounded picture of them in your mind, you will know how they speak and, by listening to their "voices", be able to reproduce them on paper.

The paradox of dialogue

Dialogue in a short story must read realistically. Your reader should be able to believe in it, accept it as a real exchange between real people.

In fact, it is not realistic at all. In a short story more than any other form of fiction, dialogue must be crisp and to the point (unless your character is a waffler, but even then you have to restrain them). People in real life do not talk concisely and to the point, they ramble and interrupt themselves, leave sentences unfinished and search vaguely for words. Try recording an ordinary conversation — say at a family meal — and then transcribing it to paper, and you will see what I mean.

Dialogue in a short story must be entirely relevant, even the chatter of a waffling character. There just isn't room for anything else, and irrelevancies distract and irritate the reader, who expects every word to mean something.

Provided that it does this, and flows easily and naturally, the reader will be satisfied. An impossible task? Not at all; every published story you read will have satisfied this requirement. There are two main points to remember:

a) Don't use stilted language. People abbreviate and condense words and phrases. Few people will say: "I cannot do this" — they will say: "can't". They will often drop the "I", as in "Hope you're keeping fit", and they will use colloquialisms — very important in dialogue, but make sure they're not too obscure.

b) Don't waste words. When people leave a party there is often a dithering on the doormat as they say goodbye, think of something else, make another effort to go, and so on. Either ignore this kind of situation, or report it in the narrative — humorously if you like and if it's that kind of story: "We performed the usual ritual dance at the front door . . ." Most people will recognize this and it will bring the story an extra smile, albeit a small one. Trying to show it in dialogue would quickly become boring.

Keep your dialogue strictly to essentials, though without hurrying it too much. Like good speech-makers, let the characters say what needs to be said in their own *characteristic* way — and then shut up.

Summary

1. Use dialogue wherever possible, but keep it *crisp*. Leave out unnecessary chitchat.
2. Use dialogue as *characterization* by letting each character speak differently.
3. Use abbreviations, colloquialisms, poor grammar — *if it is right for the character*.
4. Break speech to give added emphasis.
5. Weave dialogue in with action to help the flow.
6. Keep dialect "low-profile".
7. *Listen* to your character's voice.

9

Names and Titles

Naming your characters

The names of characters are as important as a physical description.

How often have you been introduced to someone and thought (or said): "Yes, you look *exactly* like a Mark" — or a Diana, or whatever. And when you read a name in a story, don't you immediately have a picture of that person in your mind?

Names can give you the essence of a character in just one word. Jane is plain, down to earth, a no-nonsense kind of girl; Fenella will be quite different, glamorous, lively, perhaps not entirely trustworthy. John is invariably the solid, dependable type, Julian rather more arty and sophisticated.

You may not agree with these assessments, which are my own personal reactions — especially if you know a *femme fatale* called Jane and a fat, frumpish Fenella. But if I were to list all the names I could think of in a similar fashion, I would expect you to agree with a high proportion of them. And there are sound reasons for this.

The influence of names

Since childhood, most of us have been subjected to similar influences. Our parents and teachers have read to us from the same general range of books. We have seen the same films, watched the same TV programmes. Because names are generally assigned to specific characters, we come to associate those characters with the same traits.

That's a simplification, but I believe it accounts partly for the fact that we do, in general, have similar expectations of various names. But we can go further than that.

Because these names have their own connotations, parents have tended to choose a name that will suit the person they hope their child will become. And because parents' expectations have such a powerful influence on children, particularly in the early years, there is a good chance that the child *will* grow up at least partly in the image they have (unconsciously) set. Plus the fact that its name will indicate those characteristics to other people as well, and we do tend to reflect other people's expectations.

So a baby named John because his parents want a serious, dependable son will be seen as serious and dependable by others — and will, as probably as not, grow up to be just that. Unless either expectations change or his own personality rebels, in which case he is more likely to be called Jack or Johnnie. . . .

And because this has been going on for as long as people have been using names, the whole thing has become ingrained in our culture and acts as an automatic indication of character. We don't even have to think about it. We all *know* that Dolly is likely to be vivacious and bubbling, Diana glamorous and ethereal (she was a goddess, after all), Susan sensible and practical. George will be so reliable as to be dull, Robert a tower of strength in a crisis, William probably rather pompous. All right, so you know people with all these names and they aren't a bit like that. I refuse to retract a word of it. In real life, none of them may match up to these expectations (though I'll be surprised if at least one doesn't) — *but in fiction they do*.

So this is one consideration that you must give to naming your characters. You may even find it difficult, if not impossible, to proceed with the story without doing so. For some time I wanted to use the name "Alix" for a heroine in a story. But when I tried, she never came to life and I was always forced to find a different name. It wasn't until my seventh romantic novel that I found the right story for her.

Clearly, Alix represented a particular girl, so specific that she would fit into only one mould. No doubt this applies equally to every character I use, since I have long lists and often have to go through them to find the name that "fits".

It is not a question of picking one out at random, although it can also happen that a name can come into my mind and insist on being used — such as Harriet, in another book. Harriet was a name that I had never especially liked and which never featured on my lists. But for that girl, it was the only one that would do.

If your character's name is not right, you will never have a clear picture of him or her in your mind — and you will not be able to get him or her across to your reader.

Age, background, fashion

Make sure that your characters have names within their correct age-ranges. I once listened to a story about a girl called Maud, taking place just before one of the two world wars, and was convinced it was set in Edwardian times. Nothing rang true until I found it was actually set in the late 1930s, and it took some time before I realized why I had been mistaken.

Interestingly, others listening had been under the same impression. We had all, without realizing it, associated the name Maud with an earlier decade and subconsciously transferred the entire action to that time. Later, on looking at a list of names and when they were in most common use, I discovered that Maud would indeed have been used for children born in the first and second decades of the century — yet until then I had never consciously thought about it.

Equally, hearing a story about a wife called Edith, we all took it for granted that she was in late middle age. It was disconcerting to find that Edith was in her twenties, and the discovery destroyed that precious suspension of disbelief — the reader's active co-operation with the writer — which is so essential.

In both cases, the writer was of the generation which saw those names as the names of young women. Neither had consciously realized that the names now sound old-fashioned, nor that listeners would subconsciously attribute them to much older people. So it is not only to the influences to which we ourselves have been subject that we must pay attention. We must also look at names as seen by other generations.

To me, Ann is a cool, elegant, self-contained name which exactly fitted a friend. I was dismayed at her decision to call herself Annie, a name which conjured up visions of an ancient, hobbling retainer. This, she told me brutally, simply gave away my own age — to younger people, Annie is youthful, nubile, and probably blonde. And this was the image with which she felt happier.

There is a fashion in names as in everything else. The old stalwarts — John, Elizabeth, Andrew, Sarah — seem to go on from generation to generation, so you are safe in using them. But if you want something different, keep a careful eye on the births column. And remember that the births column you want may be today's, or it may be that of twenty or thirty years ago . . .

Some fashions result in a "bulge" of names — Stephen shot to popularity in the 1960s, closely followed by Philip and Martin, so that almost every boyfriend our daughters had seemed at one time to be called either Martin or Steve (our son is Philip). For girls, it was Julie, Deborah (often spelt Debra in an attempt to make it slightly different) or Beverley.

My own school friends all seemed to be Rosemary or Margaret, with a sprinkling of Lindas, and in an earlier generation it was Lily or Nellie for girls, Harry for boys.

Look out for these and the inevitable reaction. When parents realized that Stephens and Debbies were as thick on the ground as windfall apples, they looked for something "different" — which became the next bulge (Wayne, Sharon and Tracy).

Not everyone will follow fashion. Some parents (and you should be aware of your character's parents and background) will prefer something more unusual, something distinctive. Here, even more, you will have the parents' influence making itself felt on the child's character. The father who calls his son George will be tacitly accepting the fact that his son will merge into the background of his contemporaries, and will probably not seek to influence him to any great extent. But parents who splash out with a name like Damian, or Tamara, will probably be strong-minded enough to withstand any adverse comments — and will pass on their strong-minded individuality to their child.

Don't name a minor, submissive type of character in an unusual, striking way. The reader will be constantly expecting him or her to do something startling.

With names, too, class still rears its ugly head, even if you prefer to call it socio-economic grouping. Sharon and Tracy, who started off in the middle brackets, will now be found mostly in council houses. And Sarah, Elizabeth and Caroline are still the choices made by "top" people. Look at any births column in *The Times* and you will see.

Old-fashioned names are making a comeback. Abigail, once a very "below-stairs" name, enjoyed a sudden surge in popularity a few years ago. Lucy, Emma, Charlotte and Emily, which almost died away, are back again. But will Agatha ever be resurrected? And what about Mabel, Doris and Enid? Will they ever gain ascendancy over such exotics as Gemma, Kirstie or Zara?

Religion and race

Some names have retained popularity because of their religious associations. Jews generally use Hebrew names, familiar to us all from the Bible — Ruth, Esther, Jacob. Many of these names are in general use as well, but if you give a Jewish character a non-Hebrew name it should be for a specific reason: that his parents wish to play down their Jewishness.

Roman Catholics use saints' names, and there is a wide variety — you aren't restricted to Stephen, Paul and Mary.

Puritans in the sixteenth and seventeenth centuries gave their children names like Praise-the-Lord, which must have been quite a mouthful when calling them in for tea. Today, sports-mad fathers will sometimes name their sons after entire football teams, with scant consideration for the form-filling of later life, and I know one man who only just escaped being christened Jubilee.

If you are using foreign characters, then of course you must find the right names for them, and this can be a problem. It is too easy inadvertently to choose a name that, although of the right nationality, is wrong for one of the reasons outlined above. I usually look in credit lists in the *Radio Times* or *TV Times*, finding foreign films or plays with characters of about the right age — you get two chances, both from the name of the character and that of the actor. Keep such lists in a file in case you should ever need them.

Regional British characters can be given added flavour by the use of the right name. Scots, Irish or Welsh names are relatively easy, but try to steer away from the over-common Dai, Paddy or Jock. There are plenty of interesting, colourful names — Caradoc, for instance, for your Welsh hero, Grainne for an Irish girl, Keir and Isla for the Scots couple.

Don't choose anything too outlandish, though. As a reader, I always dislike names that are phonetically obscure. I like to be able to hear the name in my mind — and if I don't know how to pronounce it, it will bother me all through the story.

"Black" names can be seen as a category on their own, for they often do not follow the rules that have evolved for "white" names. In America, many black parents tend to choose more unusual names for their children, and this trend seems to be followed in Britain's communities of Afro-Caribbean origin. Again, this is something we know almost subconsciously — these days the names Luther or Winston are more likely to be used by black parents, who still have a tendency to name children after celebrities or leaders. White parents — particularly British ones — almost fight against any such interpretation of their choice of names, although this has not always been the case. But white parents are generally more conservative anyway — they seldom invent bold, new names. Black parents are quite unabashed about giving their babies colourful names like Tamekia, Ayanna or Jamal, often of African origin.

These are names used by black Americans or West Indians. Different names will be used by Moslems or other races that now live in Britain, and these will be confined to their own traditions.

Surnames

Your characters will have surnames as well as forenames, and these too need careful thought. Although there will be fewer connotations to a surname (nobody chooses them for us), you will nevertheless find an emotional response to certain names which will probably be echoed in your readers.

Smith is ordinary; Hamilton-Smythe someone who wants to appear rather higher up the social scale. You can indicate your character's class (sorry, socio-economic grouping) by your choice of surname.

Surnames can still be very regional, especially in country areas. Mudge and Endicott were common names where I lived in Devon. I am now in the north and surrounded by Armstrongs and Dixons. In other parts, Birketts reign supreme.

Look in telephone directories for common local names. Conversely, make a note of those which *don't* appear — they will be filling a directory from some other part of the country.

I always take care that my characters' forenames and surnames go together, and that their initials are right. A romantic hero whose initials form the word ASS would be unfortunate. I also make sure that the main characters' names sound well together, and don't start with the same initial, and I steer clear of using names that are similar to each other — particularly important in the short story. And another romantic writer recently told me that she always makes sure that the heroine's forename will sound pleasant with the hero's surname — for when they are married!

Place names make good surnames, so look in gazetteers and road atlases. Some care is needed here, though — don't pick on a name that belongs solely to one family, probably landed gentry. And if your characters are themselves titled, be doubly careful — check up in *Debrett's*.

If your character is unpleasant or criminal, you may run the risk of offending someone who really has that name. You can't entirely avoid this risk, which is probably fairly small anyway — but if you are really concerned, use either a name that you are sure does not really exist (don't ask me how to ascertain that, though!) or one that is so common that no one could suspect you of having aimed it at any one person.

Dickens invented surnames that would reflect the characters of their owners, but unless you are writing comic stories this is now outdated and unnecessary. But there are quite a lot of colourful names that have fallen out of use. You can find them in parish registers and on gravestones — I once came across the remains of Susannah Cowmeadow, and felt I knew exactly what she looked like. No doubt she will find her way into a story one day.

Titles

Giving your story a title is like handing a fish bait. It is the first thing your reader sees, and it may make all the difference between tempting them to read further, and causing them to turn the page.

A title should contain the essence of the story, without giving away too much. It should, if possible, convey the tone of the story. "Gnome, Sweet Gnome" has to be humorous. "The Solution" is rather more enigmatic, but it hints at a mystery. The fact that it is also the answer to the mystery is not apparent until the end — a pleasurable factor that should apply to most stories of mystery or suspense, and makes titles for these probably the hardest to think up.

It often seems that there is only one **right** title for a story. It may hit you between the eyes straight away, or you may have to search for it. "Gnome, Sweet Gnome" was obvious. "The Solution", obvious though it seems, took a while to arrive at. First of all, I called the story "Murder By Contact" — not nearly so succinct.

Occasionally a title comes out of the blue and demands a story to be written around it. *Wildtrack*, the title of a novel about the director of a TV documentary, came while I was filming and heard the term used for a sound-without-film recording. At the same time the cameraman, asking to have a brilliant white floodlit switched off, said casually "Kill that blonde." Immediately, a picture flashed into my mind of a blonde, lying crumpled under the single, blue-hooded lamp. I have the situation and the title — all I need to do now is write the story.

A romance about cave paintings in the Dordogne could only be called "Cave Man" — yet it was some time before I thought of it. On the other hand, I knew from the start that my book with a ballooning background had to be titled *Sky High*.

Quotations are often used for titles, and if they are apt this is a good idea. Or you can "quote" from something that actually appears in the story. A symbol can be used — "The Little Brown Jug" — but make sure this is central to the story, so that the reader will not wonder afterwards what hidden meaning he or she has missed. Or you can use something as simple as your main character's name.

Keep titles short and concrete. Evocative nouns like inheritance, conspiracy, bride, affair, night, all attract attention. Or twist a familiar saying, as I did when I called a book *Hunter's Fortune*. The transposition catches the eye and sets up the curiosity that leads the reader to investigate further.

The possessive form is also a good attention-catcher; I've used "Devil's Gold," "Lucifer's Brand" and "Carver's Bride", all short, positive, concrete titles. Once again, some came easily, others had to be worked at — to reach "Devil's Gold" I drew up two lists of possible nouns and matched them until I reached the right combination.

After all this, you may find that the editor changes your title anyway. This may not be because it wasn't right — he or she may have used a title that was very similar or possibly even the same (someone pipped me to "Rapture of the Deep"), or may just have a better idea. But don't worry about it. You've done your part. If you get to the stage of having your title changed, it can mean only one thing — your story has been accepted.

Summary

In naming your characters, consider the following points:

1. What kind of person the name suggests to *you*.
2. The character's *age*.
3. The *time* in which the story is set.
4. The character's *background* and *parentage*.
5. Fashionable "bulges".
6. Region or nationality.
7. And check unusual family names or titles!

Story titles:

1. A title should express the *essence* of the story.
2. A title can sometimes give you the *idea* for a story.
3. Apt *quotations* or *sayings* can make good titles.
4. Titles should be kept *short*.
5. Use evocative and concrete *nouns* in titles.
6. And don't be upset if the editor changes your title!

10

Stories and Their Markets

You will probably already have an idea of what kind of story you want to write. We are naturally attracted to certain forms — one writer may be interested only in romance, another in horror. Or you may just want to write "stories" and not have settled on any particular form.

Whatever you want to write, getting it published will depend on the market — see Market study, below. And if you want your story to be published, you will have to tailor your writing to what editors are looking for.

Write what you enjoy

By far the biggest market is in women's magazines, and in many people's minds that means romance. Boy meets girl, boy loves girl, boy loses girl, boy gets girl back. However, many magazines today are publishing what used to be called the "general" short story — the story that doesn't involve romance. This gives writers much more scope.

Study magazines to see what kind of story they favour, and classify them — romantic, domestic, humour, suspense, etc. See how many characters generally appear, whether the story is told in the first person or the third, whether the main characters are male or female. Count the words — some magazines won't go over 1,000 words, others take stories of up to 5,000. Is the ending invariably happy, or do they allow a downbeat or open-ended finish? What is the sexual content — explicit, gentle or non-existent? Do the stories feature children or animals, or would you expect them to appeal more to the career girl?

Now try your hand at writing the ones you most enjoy reading.

Enjoying your writing is important. After all, it's why you started in the first place, isn't it? (If it's not, and you are just after a quick nickel, forget it. Editors can spot insincere writing a mile off, and they'll send it straight back.)

If you don't enjoy what you are writing, it will become a burden to you, something you drag through and are thankful to finish. If you find yourself feeling like that, stop. It may be that you are tired or unwell, or just not in the mood. In which case, you may come back to it refreshed if you give yourself a break.

But if you realize that it is because your heart really isn't in what you're writing, put it away and try something else. Perhaps later you'll find that it was your treatment that was wrong — a fresh approach may do the trick. But you may realize that you were trying to force yourself into a mould that just didn't fit.

If I feel a slight regret when approaching the end of a story, I know that my writing is probably good. Finishing should bring satisfaction — but if you are so immersed in the story that you don't want to finish it, the chances are that the reader will feel that too. She *will* finish it, of course — but her enjoyment while reading it will be remembered and she'll look out for your name again.

So write what you enjoy and your pleasure will transmit itself to your reader. Force yourself to write something you don't really like and your dislike and boredom will also come over. But the reader won't go along with you in these — she'll just flip over the page and read something else instead.

Romantic stories

Even the lightest of romantic stories must be written with sincerity, a genuine belief in the characters and what is happening to them. It's true that as we grow older we realize that teenage love usually doesn't last and will be seen later not to be so very important after all. But while we are experiencing it, it *is* intense, it *is* important. If you are writing about a teenager's first experience of romance, remember your own and give it all the intensity of emotion you went through.

The same applies to every story you write. If you don't believe in it — if you don't feel the emotions your characters are feeling — the reader won't either. It is what *you* put into the story that the reader takes out.

Most magazine romances are fairly light, but they do vary from one magazine to another. Look at the way a magazine introduces itself and its stories to find out what they want. *Woman's Weekly*, for instance, calls its stories "poignant", "tender", "nostalgic". This is a broad enough hint for any writer to take. You won't find kitchen-sink drama here, or love on the dole.

Try to look for a fresh angle on a romantic story. Attractive settings can help — setting a story in a place where a reader may have been or would like to go on holiday will provide a pleasant break from nappies and the rain running down the windows. Interesting backgrounds — a girl working at an unusual job, for instance — will also appeal. But many stories are about ordinary people, the kind of people the reader can identify with, in the kind of situations they might themselves experience. Real characters, lively dialogue and a satisfying end will get you more sales than the most exotic of settings.

Romance isn't confined to the young and single. Older people can feature in a romantic story too, but make sure your target magazine is aimed at older women. There is no point in sending a story of middle-aged love to *Jackie*.

Nostalgia

Old people frequently feature in nostalgic stories. A young girl might come to her grandmother for comfort the day before her wedding, causing the old woman to think back to her own pre-wedding nerves. A child's game will remind his grandfather of times gone by. An elderly lady might remember the day her young soldier husband left to go to war.

These are usually very gentle stories, told almost as if seen through a cloud of muslin. Edwardian times seem to be the most popular for this kind of story, and if you feel in tune with that period it might be worth trying.

Confession stories

The market for confession stories is much smaller than it was a few years ago, but does still exist and might at any time enjoy a resurgence. I have discussed the structure of the confession story in Chapter 5, but here are a few more pointers.

Confession stories are always told in the first person, in a very unliterary style — in the tone of voice of the narrator, but without recourse to dialect or accents. They always revolve around one flaw in the narrator's character, the situation this flaw brings about and its eventual resolution.

Basically, that's it. But the changes you can ring around this simple formula are numberless. When I was writing confession stories, I reckoned to write at least one a day — and sell 80 per cent of them. I was able to do this because the market was so good at that time, and because the stories appeared without a by-line — that is, without an author's name. It was not uncommon to have several stories in one issue of a magazine, and because I wrote for several I could go into a newsagent's shop at any time and know that my stories appeared in at least one and probably five or six magazines on sale.

This sounds as if I were some kind of production line, churning out stories as a factory turns out biscuits. But each story, as I wrote it, became my own small world. And at the end of a day's writing, I would be emotionally drained.

What kind of plots did I use? As I indicated in Chapter 3, it was possible to use one situation in several ways. I did this only rarely, however — not all situations would stand it. But one situation which could be so used is that of the grandfather who had lost contact with his grandchild. Each party has a point of view, which makes a story.

There was the girl who fell in love with her boyfriend's father, and the mother who fell for her daughter's boyfriend. The woman who was prejudiced against the homeless family who "squatted" next door — until they saved her house from burning down. The girl who was at the end of her tether and in danger of battering her baby.

You can deal with serious problems in a confession story. I wrote about obscene telephone callers, poison-pen letters, surrogate motherhood and the problems facing a white girl who falls in love with a black boy.

I also wrote short-short stories — under 1,000 words — which I called "thinkies". These were generally told entirely through the thoughts of the narrator: a girl on New Year's Eve, thinking back to the previous year when her boyfriend had been killed in an accident on his way home, and looking at the baby she has borne since: a new mother reflecting just after her baby's birth on the fact that she and her husband so nearly split up: a mother secretly attending the school prizegiving of a child that she had given up for adoption.

For these stories especially, you must keep up to date with current affairs. Social changes bring about new possibilities for stories; a lot of them need delicate handling, but editors who want to reflect life today will welcome them. Look for emotion. Where there is emotion, there is a story.

Getting published

Once you have written your story, you want to get it published. Don't be one of those writers who write "for themselves alone" and never send anything out. As a writer, you are a communicator. A story teller. Your job isn't finished until someone has read what you have written.

Some writers never send their work for publication, but enter competitions instead, thinking that this might be an easier route to acknowledgement. That's fine. Some competitions offer very good prizes, and it will give you confidence to win one. But sending your story to a magazine is entering a competition too — a competition with all the other writers who happen to send work to that magazine at the same time.

And the prizes in this sort of competition are just as good. You get paid. Your name gets known to editors. And your story is read by thousands, possibly millions of people.

There is nothing quite so pleasurable as sitting on a train and seeing someone enjoying a story you have written.

Market study

Sending your story out for publication is like taking produce to a market-place. You need to study your market before taking your goods along. There would be little point in taking your freshly killed meat to a market which dealt entirely in vegetables and fruit. The same applies to writing for publication.

Preferably, your market study should be done even before you begin to write. Many beginners don't do this; they sit down to write a story, then look around for somewhere to sell it. What they are looking for then is a magazine which publishes stories of exactly the length, style and content of the one they have written — which can narrow the field down to nothing. Whereas it should be quite possible to write a short story which is tailored to the requirements of a certain magazine — 3,000 words instead of 5,000, written in the first person instead of the third. If it's rejected, you look for another magazine with similar requirements — and if you can't find one, you look again at your story.

Market study is not something you do once in a lifetime. It is an ongoing procedure, which you do all the time to keep up with current trends and demands. Buy magazines regularly and study them. Especially, buy new magazines as soon as they appear on the stalls. And contribute to one of the freelancers' newsletters that often have advance information on what editors are looking for.

When you buy a magazine, don't simply read the stories — that will only tell you what the editor liked several weeks, or even months, ago.

Look as well at the rest of the magazine, especially the readers' letter pages and the advertisements. These will tell you what kind of reader the magazine is aimed at — and from this, you can deduce what kind of story might be accepted.

It should be quite clear that a magazine like *People's Friend* or *My Weekly*, aimed at the young-middle-aged or older woman with a family, is not likely to accept a gruesome horror story. Nor will a glossy like *Woman's Journal* or *Company* be interested in the kind of first-person confession that would be taken by *True Story* or *Romance*. With the in-between story, less well defined, it may be a little more difficult to judge. But reading of each magazine over a period should give you the feeling for it.

The magazines themselves do their best to help you — after all, they want their potential readers to recognize them. Look at the flags they fly on their covers. *Annabel* calls itself 'Today's Magazine For Today's Woman'. So they will be interested in other things as well as romance — "today's woman" in *Annabel*'s view is probably a young-to-middle-aged mum with either a job or some absorbing interests outside the home, rather than a high-powered and dedicated career girl. So she will be likely to enjoy stories with a domestic as well as a career slant.

Try writing to the editor and asking what kind of stories she or he is looking for. Some will supply you with "tip-sheets" which give hints as to what they want — or don't want. (Even detailed market study can fail to reveal that a certain magazine will not include any story that shows its characters smoking.) They will tell you their house style and taboos, as well as the length of story required and the kind of characters it should contain.

Radio, too, is a good market for the short-story writer. BBC Radio 4 broadcasts a short story each weekday morning — something like 250 stories a year, as opposed to the magazines which may take only twelve a year (monthlies) or 100 (weeklies). Some of the radio stories are classics, but there is still a good market for the present-day writer, and the themes vary widely.

Radio stories have their own specific requirements, and you can get the BBC's *Writing for Radio* booklet which explains them. But this doesn't mean a story written for radio won't find a home in a magazine: "Gnome, Sweet Gnome" was originally written with Radio 4's "Morning Story" slot in mind and to the length required (2,150 words). It came back with the word "amusing" pencilled on the title page — so why not let the nation laugh? I wondered — and I then sent it to *Annabel*, who accepted it.

Rejections

Everybody gets rejections. Don't be an arrogant writer like someone I knew who, having had one rejection, sent a haughty note with his next submission demanding an explanation. If what you receive with your returned manuscript is a rejection slip, look on it as an opportunity to try another magazine, and send your story out again *the same day*. Don't let it lie around the house gathering dust; nobody is going to see it there.

Don't be disheartened. Stories can be rejected for many reasons. The editor may have just accepted a story which is very similar in theme, setting or treatment. He or she may simply have enough stories on hand at present and not be accepting anything, however good. He or she may simply not like your story — the judgement is bound to be partly subjective. (I once had several stories refused by an editor — but when a new fiction editor was taken on and I sent in the same stories again, they were all taken at once.)

Your market study may be at fault — check to see that you are sending your work to the right magazine, that you are not missing some obvious point which could make all the difference.

Or you may have to face the fact that it really isn't good enough. In which case, you try, try again. Writing is like a muscle. Exercise it, and you must improve.

Sometimes an editor will scribble something on your rejection slip. I sent "The Solution" to a glossy monthly and received a rejection slip which told me the story was well written, but not quite suitable for that particular magazine, and suggested other markets. If this happens to you, it is an excellent sign (albeit not quite as good as being accepted!). It means that the editor liked your work enough to take the trouble to encourage you. Send her or him something else quickly, taking the advice into account.

Even better, you may get a letter with your story. This happened when I sent "The Solution" to *Woman's Own*. This particular magazine was at that time not encouraging any submissions (a fact of which I was unaware — my market study slipping up!) — and had recently run a short-story competition. Nevertheless, the fiction editor wrote me a charming and friendly letter, saying that although she liked my story she could not accept it because she already had quite a few that concerned women disposing of domineering husbands. She asked me to send other stories and told me what she was looking for at that time.

Some editors (and the editors of D.C. Thomson magazines are well known for this) will go to great lengths to help you get your story into publishable shape. They will send it back with a detailed criticism, telling you where you have gone wrong and suggesting ways of putting it right. When you get this kind of editorial help, drop everything and rewrite your story to their advice. I know many writers who owe their start to these helpful editors, and this advice and encouragement is invaluable. But don't demand it, or write and ask why they rejected your story. Editors are busy people and don't enjoy being pestered.

Editors are inundated with stories every day, many of them useless, many more of publishable standard. They can take only a limited number, and if they take the trouble to write *anything* (even "amusing") on your rejection slip, it should be taken as a very encouraging sign. Write more for editors who do this, and keep your name in their minds. Eventually, your persistence must pay off.

Short-story collections

Writers frequently ask how to get their short stories published as collections, in a book. Obviously, this is possible — one does see such collections in libraries. But a look at them will soon tell you that it is rare for publishers to accept a collection from a new author.

Often, a collection of short stories will not even be written by one person; they are more likely to be stories by various authors around a theme, such as crime. Other volumes may be of stories by established writers, many of them already published in magazines. Or they may be stories written by a well-known novelist or established short-story writer.

It is not impossible for a collection of short stories by an unknown writer to be accepted by a publisher. You will find addresses of the publishers who do publish such collections in the *Writers' & Artists' Yearbook*. But, meanwhile, why not continue to send your stories to magazines? You have nothing to lose but your postage.

Summary

1. Write what you enjoy.
2. *Feel* the emotions your characters experience — if you can't identify with them, neither will your reader.
3. Study your market and decide which magazine you are aiming at before you begin to write.

4. Don't be disheartened by rejections. Send your story out again at once.
5. Always follow an editor's suggestions.

11

The Nitty-gritty

You have now written your story and want to send it out for publication. How do you go about this?

Preparing your manuscript

First of all, it must be typed. Editors are too busy and value their eyes too much to wade through pages of sprawling, or even neat, handwriting.

It doesn't have to be perfectly typed — nobody will reject a manuscript simply because of the odd mistake — but it should be tidy and not covered with handwritten corrections. One or two a page can be permitted, but any more and it begins to look a mess.

Typewriters can be bought reasonably cheaply — you can get some very good second-hand standards — but if you intend to do a lot of writing, buy the best you can afford. A good strong manual is better than a low-priced electric model that is intended for only a few letters a week. A good electric model is even better, an electronic positive luxury. Or you can go into word processing — of which more in the next chapter.

Use good-quality white typing paper of A4 size, type in double-spacing on one side only, and KEEP A COPY. Don't try to cram too much on a page; editors need wide margins all round for instructions to the printer. I generally type 25 lines to a page, with 70 characters to a line, which seems to be quite acceptable. It makes it easier to count the number of words, too.

Number each page — I was surprised when judging a competition recently to find just how many writers didn't — and put your name and address on the first and last pages.

Your title-page will consist of your name and address in the top right-hand corner, as on a letter. (But don't add the date.) Include your telephone number, in the top left-hand corner. In the centre of the page type the title, in block capitals, with your name or pen-name, underneath.

Towards the bottom, on the left, type the number of words in the story — rounded, not exact (the mark of an amateur). On the right, type the letters FBSR, which stand for First British Serial Rights. (I'll explain this more fully in a few minutes.)

Put it into an envelope — get one large enough to take the paper unfolded, as folding soon makes it look tatty — and include a second envelope of the same size, with the correct amount of postage on it, addressed to yourself. You will soon learn to tell, as soon as you see the second envelope coming back, whether the story has been accepted or not. If it hasn't, you'll be glad to have a still-tidy manuscript to send to the next editor on your list — though it is a good idea to retype the title page, to keep it looking fresh and new — and if it has you won't mind the expense of a big envelope.

Include a brief covering letter with the story. It is worth finding out the name of the fiction editor so that you can address the envelope and letter to her or him by name. Don't go into any details: a simple "I enclose my story 'Gnome, Sweet Gnome' for your consideration and hope that you will find it suitable for inclusion in *Gnome's Weekly* is all you need. Later, you may find the editor addressing you by your first name and signing with hers or his. But let them make the first move; editors don't much like over-familiar contributors.

Rights and copyright

Now let's go back to those letters FBSR. These indicate that you are offering the right to publish the story for the first time in this country (and in other countries, such as Australia, in which the same edition of the magazine appears). The magazine cannot publish it a second time (unlikely anyway) or sell it abroad or to a different publication without asking your permission and offering a further fee.

This is important for short stories, which are often syndicated. As a beginner, I once received an acceptance for World Rights (you may also be offered payment for All Rights) which I agreed and then regretted. On my next sale to that particular magazine I refused World Rights and stipulated First British Serial Rights only — and found myself being paid the same amount, and keeping my copyright.

Keeping your copyright entitles you to offer the story for sale a second time, either in this country or abroad, so long as you say which rights have already been sold. You may also find after you have made a few sales to the same magazine, or even to the same "house", that you are approached by a syndication agency, offering to sell your work abroad. The agency may have close ties with the publishing house itself and if so will be quite reputable. All you have to do is say "yes" — and wait for the cheques.

Or you may find an agent who is willing to handle your work, either in

Britain or abroad. In this case, you will have to pay commission on sales, but it could well be worth it. You can find some addresses in *The Writers' & Artists' Yearbook*.

Don't worry about translation — you won't be expected to send versions of your story in French or German. Somewhere between here and there is a nest of translators, beavering away at translating stories for Helga and Jeannette to read. For you, the money will come as a welcome bonus to what your story has already earned.

Keeping a record

Once you begin to send stories out, it is important to keep track of them. Everyone has their own way of doing this, and you will probably evolve your own. Here is mine.

I use a hard-backed exercise book, which I rule across and down in columns, headed thus:

| | *Title* | | |
| *Magazine* | *Date sent* | *Accepted/Rejected* | *Payment* |

Each story has its own page, or half-page, so there is plenty of room for a long list of magazines if the story proves difficult to place. The "date sent" for the second time out will also indicate how long the first editor kept it, and so on. The Accepted/Rejected column need not be very wide, since A or R will suffice, and in the Payment column I write the amount offered for the story and tick it when payment is received.

This system has worked well for me; you may prefer to use something different. But you must keep some kind of log-book, or within a very short time you will find yourself in a state of total confusion.

Money matters

Take a businesslike approach to your writing. Even if you consider it a hobby, others are making part of their living from it; editors wouldn't hold their jobs if no stories came in. So, as well as your log, you should keep accounts.

Short-story writing is not especially expensive, but even before you sell that first story you will have incurred some expense. Your typewriter, or typing charges; stationery; postage; pens or pencils; telephone calls and part of the rental; magazines, newspapers; books to help you with your writing such as this book, dictionaries and encyclopaedias; research and travel expenses, to search out background information. Keep them all noted down, and keep all receipts. And ask for proper ones — a till listing isn't always good enough.

You should also notify the Inland Revenue once you begin to receive payment. Earnings from writing are assessed under Schedule D, and even if you have no other income the Inland Revenue should be informed. They will be, anyway, by the magazines you sell to, so you may as well get in first and impress them with your honesty.

You will probably be asked to return accounts at the end of each fiscal year (that's early in April) and this is when you will be glad you kept that record of expenses. It may keep you below the taxable limit or, if you have earned well, it will keep your tax bill down. You may even find that it is higher than your payments — in which case you think again about short-story writing as a lucrative hobby. (But don't be discouraged too soon — many writers take a long time to get started and then shoot to the top like rockets. The stories of famous writers who could paper the walls with rejection slips are legion.)

If you can see that you are going to have to pay income tax, it is only common sense to keep back some of the money you earn. Perhaps it will be about a quarter or a third of your earnings. Put that amount in a separate account — preferably one that will earn interest — with *each payment you receive*. In this way, you will always know just what money is yours and won't overspend.

Summary

1. Always type your manuscript, using double-spacing with good margins all around, on A4 paper.
2. Keep your copyright.
3. Keep a record of submissions.
4. Keep accounts, and tell the taxman (but don't forget to charge realistic expenses).

12

A Word about Word Processors

The word processor is an animal that has crept into the writer's world comparatively recently. Only five years ago, few had heard the term and even fewer understood what it meant. Even now, there is a lot of confusion.

It is not my intention to go deeply into word processing — you can buy a companion book in this series which will fully explain the concept and how it affects the writer. But it seems to me that no writing manual today would be complete without a brief explanation, from which you can decide whether or not you want to investigate more fully.

What is a word processor?

A word processor comes in several forms — this is what makes it so confusing. Probably, you would be quite happy with any one of them. But there is bound to be one that would suit you best, and it is worth searching for that one.

First, let's see what it will do for you. After all, if you're buying a car you think first of what you want it to do: carry you from place to place. It's only after you've made that decision that you look at its component parts.

There is no doubt that a word processor will make writing easier for you. No, it won't think up ideas, structure your plot, express your characters more vividly or write amusing dialogue. But it will, by freeing you from a lot of purely mechanical actions, help you to do all these things; it will free your mind and enable you to get on with the job of writing. And it will produce a perfect copy for you to send to an editor.

You don't have to be an expert typist to use a word processor. In fact, the poorer a typist you are, the more valuable it will be to you. Nor do you have to be a computer genius or an electronic whizz kid. Do you know exactly how your old typewriter works?

You don't have to learn a strange new "language" (although you'll inevitably pick up some jargon) and you don't have to learn to do your own programming. The word processor, to the writer, is no more complicated than a pencil. It is a tool; not an end in itself.

What you will have, when you sit down with a word processor on your desk, is:

A keyboard, exactly as you have on your typewriter, but with some extra keys.

A computer which contains a word-processing program.

A Visual Display Unit (hereafter referred to as a VDU), looking similar to the screen of a small, portable television.

A storage system which will consist of either disks or tape cassette. (These disks are not for playing pop songs, but for storing your work. Generally known as "floppy" disks to differentiate them from the "hard" disk which some bigger machines use, they are either 5¼" or 3" in diameter and are inserted in your computer when you begin work. Some are single-sided, some double-sided, some double-density, and as you might suppose this refers to their various storage capacities.)

A printer, which is really the "other half" of your typewriter.

All you do is type on the keyboard. Instead of the words appearing on paper in front of you, they will appear on the screen. And here is the beauty of the word processor — all those mistakes you make, all those typing errors, spelling mistakes, poor sentences, unfortunate juxtapositions — all can be altered by the touch of a key. You can overwrite, erase, insert, move text to your heart's content. One key will underline, another will sort out an untidy paragraph so that each line is "justified" and ends neatly down the margin, another will enable you to hyphenate a long word.

To a writer, the word processor is magic. If you want to change a character's name, it will find each place in which the name occurs and replace it with the one you want. I once used the name Alistair and until I read what I had written wasn't even aware that the name had several different spellings — let alone that I knew and had used them all! I didn't have my word processor then and the task of sifting through an entire novel was laborious and time-consuming, with the added danger that I might have missed some. The word processor would have done the job in minutes — and found them all.

As you write, your work is stored on the disk or cassette. It is then safe. And although I have heard horror stories of writers "losing" work, this has never happened to me, nor — with reasonable care — should it. But to make absolutely sure, I copy it on to a fresh disk so that I have two versions, the one I am working with and my "back-up".

I always print out a copy of my first draft, as I like to sit down with paper and read it through, making corrections and alterations in pen as I go. I then return to my word processor and "call up" the work on to the screen to make the corrections on to my disk. This takes only a few minutes each morning and refreshes my memory, getting me back into the atmosphere of my work. I may need to go through the procedure again, but in general that will be my final draft. But however many drafts are needed, the word processor makes the task infinitely simpler — and even enjoyable.

Some writers like to work entirely on the screen, never printing out until they are completely satisfied.

Whichever way you work, when you come to print out your final copy there is nothing easier. You simply insert the paper in your printer, press the keys which will tell the computer to print out, and leave it alone — coming back later to a perfectly printed copy which any editor will be glad to receive. And if rewriting is necessary, the drudgery is cut to a fraction.

Choosing your word processor

One of the deciding factors is price.

My own system is based on a microcomputer (a British Micro Mimi 803), with 64K RAM (the memory capacity) and double disk drive. I have a Philips monitor (that's the screen, which sits on top of the computer itself) and an Adler daisy-wheel printer which is basically an Adler electronic typewriter minus its keyboard, though it does have other refinements, including its own "memory", which are essential for it to work with the computer. My only software is the Wordstar word-processing program, but I could if I liked use my computer for all kinds of other activities — data storage (which could be useful for research), graphics, mathematics, accounts and a multitude else.

One of the most useful features of this particular machine is that it has a row of 17 *function* keys as well as the normal typing keys. These keys act as a "control" and enable the computer to carry out various commands within the program which I am using at the time (Wordstar). When these function keys are absent, or fewer, as is the case with many computers, you will use a "control" key (which I also have). This key, pressed in conjunction with a normal "letter" key, will command the function you require. My function keys simply mean that I don't have to remember the various combinations of keys — instead, I have assigned to them various functions: "delete character", "delete word", "delete line", "move text", "underline", "set margins", "centre text", "find and replace", etc. I just have to press the right key for the right function and it will be carried out instantly.

I can assign two functions to each key. And on each of the nine *numeric* keys which I have in a block beside my alphabet keys, I can write a whole phrase, such as a name and address, so that when it is pressed the entire thing — up to 250 characters — is automatically typed. Very useful for foreign phrases or words about which I have a mental block!

I use two disks together. One has Wordstar on it — this is the word-processing program which will do all these useful things. There are various other programs, all claiming to be best, some of them unique to one particular make, so what you use will probably depend on the system you buy.

My second disk has the current book, story or article I am writing. I find that one disk will take approximately half of a 55,000-word novel, although I usually use three disks per book — this means there is plenty of room for rewriting, should it be necessary. For short stories or articles, fewer disks will be needed. But you should always make a copy of every disk — it takes only a few seconds at the end of each day's work — and store them in a different place, in case of accidents.

You can reuse disks, so when you think that there will be no further need for rewriting — when the story is published — and you have a "hard" copy on paper, you can wipe it off and start again.

My printer is a full-size electronic daisy-wheel printer, which produces letter-quality printing at the rate of about one page every two to three minutes. I use 12-pitch, but this can be changed at a touch to 10 or 15. I use a nylon ribbon, which lasts for at least one book; say a book and the draft of the next one, plus any other writing — stories, letters, articles etc. — I may do in between.

My system cost me £2,500 when I bought it in 1983. That's a lot of money, but I do a lot of writing; in that time I have written the equivalent of several books, including rewrites, plus articles, short stories and letters. Before I had it, I was typing my books and then sending them for professional typing. It was six weeks before I got my manuscript back (during which time I was on hot bricks) and it cost me £100 each time. Once I had my word processor, I was able to print my final draft out in a day — and, because it speeded up my writing so much, I was able to write the book more quickly in the first place.

If you find spelling difficult, you can have an extra spelling program added in; this will highlight any word you have misspelt and give you the correction.

Dedicated word processors

These are less popular because most people will, like me, buy a system that can do other things too — and because, oddly enough, they are much more expensive.

A dedicated word processor will do just that — process words. It won't do anything else. Its program is built in and you can't buy a database program or a mathematics program to extend its capabilities. It will do the job you want it to very well, but you may find yourself paying upwards of £5,000.

You can also buy an electronic typewriter that has been extended to become a simple dedicated word processor. These too have disk drives, and the sentence you are typing is displayed on a small panel above the keyboard. There is no extra printer, the printing being done by the typewriter itself. I was quite interested in these for a while, but finally decided in favour of having a proper VDU — mine shows the full width of the page and half its depth, which is as much as you need to see. You can now buy a VDU for some of these models, but again they are *dedicated* and can't be used for anything else, and they cost about the same as my more flexible system did.

Home computers

Quite a lot of writers have looked into the use of "home computers" in word processing and have put together some useful packages. You will find more information on these in the companion books *The Magazine Writer's Handbook* and *Low-Cost Word-Processing*, both by Gordon Wells. I would only say that with a computer which uses a cassette recorder for storage, retrieval will be slow and frustrating, and it is well worth getting a disk drive. Valuable writing time can be wasted waiting for a cassette recorder to wind slowly through the tape to find the place you got to yesterday. With disk storage, it takes only seconds. Remember — time is (potential) sales!

Home computers, however, are for amateurs and games. If you are, or hope to be, a serious professional author, get professional equipment which will last. Many home computer keyboards fail after only a year or less of use and will not stand up to intensive working.

Printers

The last, but not least important, piece of equipment is your printer. And again, you have a choice — although any writer who means to tackle the job seriously will not hesitate to go for a daisy-wheel.

For a while, the dot-matrix type of printer was very popular. It is fast — it will type a page in seconds, beside which the daisy-wheel seems almost ponderous. But it is certainly less clear, each letter being made up of tiny dots, and the descenders of letters like "g" and "y" are often non-existent. Editors who didn't at first worry about them began to complain when more and more manuscripts arrived that had been printed out on dot-matrix printers, and now some are refusing to read them.

"Letter-quality" dot-matrix printers are available, but in "letter-quality" mode they are not much faster than the daisy-wheel. They will, however, produce draft-quality very quickly. But they are at present very expensive.

The daisy-wheel printer, which prints beautiful, clear type, will always be acceptable. It is slower (though it will still beat any typist) but your finished page will look as if it has been typed by an expert. And if it is a choice between reading your manuscript and one that is faint and fuzzy, with handwritten corrections all over it and an old coffee-stain decorating the title-page — well, what would you do if *you* were editor?

So what — and how — do you choose? Don't buy anything in a hurry. Consult the books mentioned above; read computer magazines; talk to people who understand word processors or, even better, people who already own one. And go and see as many as possible.

If you are going to buy a professional machine, go to a good dealer rather than a High Street shop, and make sure that the salesman understands both his product and your requirements. Ask about training in its use — I have been horrified by stories of people who have been sent home with a package they didn't know the first thing about, and left to sort it out for themselves. A good dealer will spend time with you — mine spent three full days in customizing my Wordstar program so that it exactly fitted my needs, and teaching me to use it, and was always ready to answer any further queries.

Even before you buy, the dealer should let you try out his computers, and good ones will spend some time with you, listening to what your requirements are. If they won't, steer clear of them. Better still, get them to let you have the whole system on trial for a few days.

I was lucky enough to find a dealer who would do this, and it sold me the machine. For the first day or so, I admit I was daunted — there was so much to remember, and it was so easy to go wrong. But within two days I felt sufficiently confident to try writing a letter. And by the time he returned and wrested the machine from my grasp, I had already written two chapters of my new book. . . . From then on, I couldn't wait to have my own, and my old electric typewriter seemed cumbersome and frustratingly slow.

If you are going to write books as well as short stories, you need the biggest storage capacity you can afford — a double-disk drive is essential. But if you are going to concentrate on shorter pieces of work, this is probably not so vital. You will not be storing such large chunks of work, and an expensive machine could be more than you will usefully employ.

Take your time in choosing and buying your word processor. Shop around until you are sure you know what you want. And then you should, as I and hundreds of others have, find yourself embarking on a long and happy partnership.

Summary

1. Assess your requirements, particularly with regard to storage capacity and ease of access.
2. Talk to people who already use word processors.
3. Shop around. Look at and try as many different systems as possible.
4. Go to a good dealer who will take an interest in you both before *and* *after* you buy.

13

The Writer's Library

Here are a few books which I have found helpful, and a few that you need:

Writers' and Artists' Yearbook (published annually by A. & C. Black). No writer should be without it. It lists several hundred magazines and newspapers in Britain, with a brief description of what they are interested in. If you can't find a magazine on the bookstalls, write to the editorial address and ask for a copy (sending the right amount of money and postage).

The *Yearbook* also contains information on book publishers, agents, societies, proof-reading and associated matters.

The Magazine Writer's Handbook (published in the "Writers' Guides" series by Allison & Busby), by Gordon Wells. How to do your market research, telling you what to look for, who uses what, how to submit both stories and articles, and with an appraisal of 69 magazines currently on sale. But don't let it make you lazy — use it, but do your own up-to-date research as well.

Dictionaries — every writer needs them. I have the *Concise Oxford* and the *Collins*. Keep them up to date, as the language does change.

Roget's Thesaurus. For a long time, I thought this was some sort of prehistoric animal — but it's not. I am now always consulting it. But take care — don't fall in love with it. Use the simple, understandable word rather than the obscure.

Dictionaries of Quotations — I have the *Penguin Dictionary of Quotations* and *Modern Quotations*, and the *Oxford Dictionary of Quotations*.

The Oxford Dictionary for Writers and Editors — this little book gives you rulings for spelling, capitalization, abbreviation, etc. For instance, if you want to use the word "caftan" or "cagoule" it will tell you what a caftan and a cagoule are and warn you not to spell them with a "k".

Similarly, the *Penguin Dictionary of Troublesome Words* serves as a guide to the pitfalls that can bother us all — when it is right to use "due to", how to repair a split infinitive and why the word "different" ought to be much rarer than it is.

First Names First (published by Coronet) and *Our Secret Names* (published by Sidgwick & Jackson), both by Leslie Alan Dunkling.

Fascinating information about forenames, with lists of names and when they were first used in Britain, what age groups are most likely to be known by them, and so on.

The Penguin Dictionary of Surnames (second edition published in 1978) is a guide to British surnames, showing the derivation of names (ancestral, local, occupational or descriptive).

Saints and Their Emblems in English Churches (published by Basil Blackwell), by R.L.P. Milburn. Now probably out of print, but if you can find one it is full of saints' names, from Acca to Zacharias, together with the story of each saint. If you are looking for a really unusual Christian name, this could be where you'd find it.

How to Write Short Stories that Sell, by Louise Boggess. Published by Writer's Digest Books, Cincinnati, Ohio, and available here through agencies that distribute American books, especially about writing.

Writing for Radio, available from the BBC. Tells you about the various aspects of writing for radio, including short stories.

The Complete Plain Words (published by Pelican), by Sir Ernest Gowers, revised by Sir Bruce Fraser. Originally written for civil servants (though you may think most of them have ignored it) but now read by anyone who wants to learn to write simply and directly.

Research for Writers (published by Midas Books), by Ann Hoffman. Information about museums, libraries, reference books and how to cope with your research once you've done it. Probably short-story writers won't need to research a lot, but it's useful to have on hand.

And my own favourite, a book I've had since I was fourteen and won the only prize of my scholastic career — a book token with which I bought *Performing Flea* by P.G. Wodehouse. You can get it now as the middle section of *Wodehouse-on-Wodehouse*, published by Penguin. It is a collection of letters written by Wodehouse to another writer, William Townend, and is a mine of writing know-how and practical advice. Each time I read it I am infected anew by Wodehouse's enthusiasm, and encouraged by the fact that even he had his moments of doubt and his rejections. None of which affected his generosity — he would actually think out a plot, knowing that it wasn't his kind of story, and send it to his friend for writing up.

Wouldn't we all love a few friends like that!